the Rise
of Red China

by ROBERT GOLDSTON

the Rise of

Red China

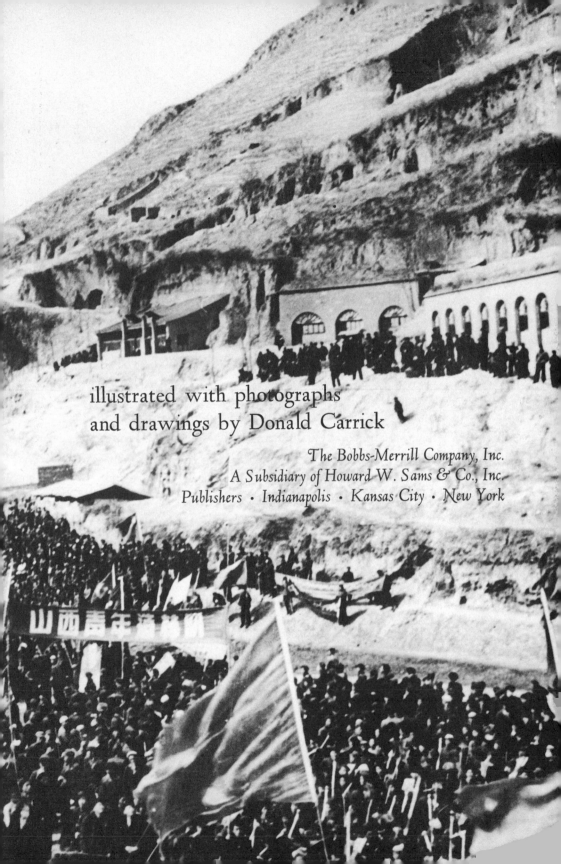

illustrated with photographs
and drawings by Donald Carrick

The Bobbs-Merrill Company, Inc.
A Subsidiary of Howard W. Sams & Co., Inc.
Publishers · Indianapolis · Kansas City · New York

The author wishes to express his gratitude to Random House, Inc., for permission to quote from Mr. Edgar Snow's *The Other Side of the River,* Random House, Inc., copyright © 1962 by Edgar Snow.

All photographs in this book are from United Press International with the exception of the following: Robert Capa-Magnum, pp. 6-7, 140-141, 146-147, 152-153, 158-159, 162-163 "Images of War" copyright © 1964, 171, 194-195; The Bettmann Archive, pp. 107, 149; Camera Press-PIX, p. 216.

The map on pages 128-129 is by Irving Weinstein.
Photographic research by Lisl Steiner.

For Theresa, *whose advent prompted it* . . .

Contents

Prologue:

News from Tartary

PERHAPS THE most surprising thing about the adventures related by Marco Polo in his book of travels was that anyone believed them, but most people did. Of course there were scoffers and these jestingly referred to Marco as *"Il Milione"*—the man who talks in millions—from his habit of insisting on the millions of people, the millions of houses, the millions of boats, the millions in treasure he had seen. Yet, from the very first, when Marco Polo, his uncle, and his father returned to their native city of Venice in the year 1295, they found a willing audience for their fabulous tales of twenty-six years in the mysterious East at the golden courts of the Great Khan. Later, while a prisoner of war at Genoa in 1298, Marco recited his adventures to one Rustichello of Pisa, a professional writer of romances who knew a best-seller when he heard it and hastened to copy them down—with modest embellishments. Truly it was a book of wonders.

"The journey had taken more than three years...."

Camel caravan waits outside the Great Wall.

The journey had taken more than three years and was in itself a catalogue of the impossible. Setting out from the Crusader city of Acre in 1273, the Polos made their way by caravan trails through lands whose very existence was only guessed at in Europe. There was the city of Shibarghan, boasting the world's finest melons; the mountains of Talkhan, "very large and all made of salt"; the land of Kashmir, whose people knew how to make their idols speak and change the weather through black magic; the town of Ishkashim, famous for its belligerent porcupines; the country of Badakhshan, where the descendants of Alexander the Great grew wealthy exploiting mountains of rubies, emeralds, and lapis lazuli; the great plain of Pamir, so high among the mountains that no birds could fly there; the "very large and splendid" city of Samarkand, with its Christian church of Saint John the Baptist, wherein a pillar of stone was miraculously supported in thin air; the great Gobi desert, where spirit voices lured the unwary traveler to his doom; the land of Ghinghintalas, where lived the fabled salamander; the country of Sinju, where the cattle were as large as elephants and "very handsome in appearance, being covered with long hair"; and the province of Tenduc, formerly part of the domains of the legendary Prester John.

Yet these marvels paled into insignificance when compared to Marco's description of the city of Kinsai (modern Hangchow), capital of southern China. Like Marco's native Venice, Kinsai was built upon lagoons of water and intersected by innumerable canals. But all of Venice (at that time the greatest city in Europe) would have fitted easily into any one of Kinsai's twelve quarters. For this city, whose very existence was unsuspected in the West, was more than one hundred miles in circumference. Its main street was two hundred feet wide and ran from one end of the city to the other, broken every four miles by large squares lined with palaces, gardens, and shops. There were (according to Marco) twelve thousand stone bridges in Kinsai and many of them were so high that full-masted seagoing vessels could pass beneath them. The city was crowded—

with lords and merchants clad in silk, with beautiful ladies carried through the streets in richly appointed litters, with shops selling pepper and spices and pearls and silks and every kind of manufactured item. There was a great lake studded with wooded islands upon which stood gaily decorated pleasure pavilions, and, not far away, a royal palace many times larger and richer than any in which a European king slept. And to Kinsai from the nearby seaport city of Zaiten (modern Ch'üan-chiao) came thousands of junks, their decks laden with spices from the Indies and rare woods such as ebony and sandalwood; part of the vast fleet with which the merchants of China traded east to Zipangu (Japan), west to India and the Arabian peninsula and even the East African coast, and south to Sumatra, Java, and Borneo. To the men of Kinsai, imperial Venice at the height of its grandeur was no more than a backwoods village—and Kinsai had been old in wealth and civilization when Venice was no more than a collection of mud huts.

Nor was Kinsai unique in the domains of the Great Khan. Not far from it stood the city of Sugui (modern Suchow), which was itself larger than Constantinople, while to the north stood the great city of Cambaluc (modern Peking) from which Kublai, who was Khan at the time of Marco Polo, administered an empire larger than all of Europe. For twenty years, Marco served the learned and genial Kublai Khan as ambassador, administrator, and trusted lieutenant, and his work carried him to nearly every corner of the Khan's dominions. But although his book faithfully records such unknown wonders as gunpowder, cannon, and compasses, it tells but little of the history of the unique people who had constructed the world's mightiest civilization. Perhaps Marco Polo, a merchant and a practical man of affairs, did not bother to acquaint himself with that history—but more likely he refrained from telling what he knew of it for fear that his readers simply would not believe it!

Who in Europe would have believed that at the time of Moses, more than fourteen centuries before the birth of Christ, a large and prosperous kingdom (Shang) existed along the Yellow River in

China whose people had mastered the arts of writing, pottery, and silk weaving? Who would have believed that when Solomon built his great temple in Jerusalem one thousand years before the advent of Christianity, the Chinese had mastered the art of irrigation and, like the Assyrians, were expert in the use of war chariots? And glass—that Venetian speciality—would not the good citizens of Venice have scoffed to learn it had been invented in China more than a thousand years before Marco Polo's journey? And what would a cultivated European of the thirteenth century have made of the facts that when Socrates drank his poison, Chinese philosophers were already beginning to understand the properties and nature of magnetism; that while Rome battled Carthage for control of the Mediterranean Sea, Chinese engineers were completing a Great Wall nearly fifteen hundred miles long to maintain control of their northwestern frontiers; that when the great library at Jerusalem was burned by the Romans and the Essenes were hiding their parchment scrolls, the Chinese had invented paper; that when the great Emperor Charlemagne was struggling to teach himself to read and write, Chinese were beginning to read printed books and government employees were being graded through civil service examinations? All things considered, it was perhaps just as well that Marco Polo did not record these facts, if he knew them.

But what Marco did set down in his wonderful book was sufficient to grip the imagination of Europeans. For example, his description of the Khan's summer palace at Shandu was translated into a dream-vision by the English poet Samuel Taylor Coleridge almost five hundred years after Marco's death:

In Xanadu did Kubla Khan
  A stately pleasure-dome decree:
Where Alph, the sacred river, ran
Through caverns measureless to man
  Down to a sunless sea.
So twice five miles of fertile ground

". . . what Marco Polo had to tell his fellow Venetians was extremely accurate." Ancient Chinese astronomical instruments.

With walls and towers were girdled round:
And here were gardens bright with sinuous rills,
*   Where blossomed many an incense-bearing tree;*
And here were forests ancient as the hills,
*   Enfolding sunny spots of greenery.*

Yet in spite of the almost magical nature of the wonders recited in his book of travels, what Marco Polo had to tell his fellow Venetians was extremely accurate. From the salt mines of Talkhan and the ruby mines of Badakhshan to the asbestos he saw thrown into the fire at Ghinghintalas and the yaks of Sinju, Marco Polo reported only the truth. And when news came of the death of Kublai Khan and the fall of the Mongol Empire in the East, when the resurgence of Mohammedan power throughout central Asia once more interrupted communication between Europe and China, men would not give up their dream of visiting Marco Polo's fabled lands. Almost two hundred years after Marco's death, a copy of his book came into the hands of a young Genoese sailor who read it avidly, making numerous notes on the margins of his copy. The sailor was seized with a burning ambition to see for himself the marvels he'd read about. And what if the land routes to the Far East were blocked by the power of Islam? Like all educated men of his day, Christopher Columbus knew that the earth was round. Therefore if one sailed west, far enough west over the expanse of unknown ocean— surely one would reach the golden courts of Cathay? As the English historian Eileen Power has pointed out, of all the marvels of Marco Polo, this was his last. "He discovered China in the thirteenth century when he was alive, and in the fifteenth, when he was dead, he discovered America!"

1

Twenty-One Dynasties

AN OLD American missionary in China once peevishly remarked about Chinese history that it was "remote, obscure, and worst of all—there is entirely too much of it!" And truly, if one reads the history of China as the record of who slew whom and who begat which emperor, then Chinese history can overmatch that of any other nation for profusion of detail, confusion of names, and sheer mass. For one of the salient facts of Chinese history is that it has been continuous: far and away the longest continuous history of any nation on earth. A second extremely important fact of Chinese history has been its isolation: until the last two centuries China has had but little contact with the outside world, and almost none with the West. For this isolation there are obvious geographical reasons. China's western land frontiers—the great deserts of central Asia and the tremendous mountain ranges of the Pamirs and the

Himalayas—were an effective barrier to all but the hardiest explorers and traders. As for the eastern seas, the poet Li Tai Po has written:

> *Immortals we shall be one day when the yellow herons*
> *   Come to bear us away on their backs.*
> *Corsairs of the open sea, we lack the courage to follow*
> *   The flight of the white gulls.*

Chinese mariners, faced by the typhoon-ridden and tempestuous China Sea and the seemingly endless Pacific Ocean to the east, turned their ships south to the Indies and west to India and Africa. Large Chinese trading stations existed on Africa's east coast, and Chinese ships were probably the best in the world from the eleventh to the fifteenth century. But just as the Portuguese began to sail down the west coast of Africa, the Ming Dynasty, deciding that large-scale trading expeditions to the west were unprofitable, brought their transocean sailing ventures to an end. Thereafter, China's sea frontiers were to remain a self-imposed barrier to be breached by Europeans.

The prehistory of China, based on such archaeological finds as the remains of "Peking Man," goes back for at least 500,000 years. And, either out of the stone-age communities along the banks of the Yellow River, or in successive waves of invasion from central Asia, the Hans, immediate ancestors of the Chinese people, gradually established control over the rich farming lands of northern and central China before the dawn of recorded history. The earliest Chinese "dynasty," partly shrouded in legend and half-mythical, the Hsia Dynasty, may have been founded as early as 2000 B.C.

The relations between the Hans and their present-day descendants, and the "barbarians" they defeated for control of China, represent one of the master keys of Chinese history. For thousands of years, intermittent warfare has continued between the Chinese and such non-Chinese races as the Kazakhs, the Min Chia, and the

Miaos within China proper, while successive assaults by Mongols, Tartars, and other borderland peoples have inflamed China's frontiers, especially in the north, for many centuries. Confucius once said: "The art of patience and learning, clemency towards criminals: these are the virtues of the men of the south who are called Sages. But sleeping on the rough hides of beasts, knowing how to die with fortitude: these are the virtues of the men of the north who are called Braves." And for thousands of years, the Chinese have patiently helped the brave barbarians both within and without China to die with or without fortitude. As recently as a century ago, under the Ching Dynasty, the last survivors of the Min Chia race met the fate of the North American Indians, semi-extermination, at the hands of Imperial forces. It was also under the Ching Dynasty that the Emperor called together all the people of the Miao tribes in order to inform them of his decrees. As the unsuspecting Miao tribes entered a mountain ravine, they were massacred by waiting Imperial troops.

Yet the greatest weapon of Chinese expansion was not conquest: it was absorption. For Confucius also said: "Let those who wear the costume of the barbarians be barbarians; those who wear the costume of the Chinese be Chinese." In other words, as the Sons of Han slowly expanded southward to the borders of present-day Viet Nam, Laos, and Burma, and westward into the high plateaus of Tibet, the peoples in their path who continued to follow barbarian ways faced extermination, but those who adopted the customs and manners of the Chinese were accepted as Chinese without discrimination.

As the Hsia Dynasty gives way to the Shang Dynasty between 1600 and 1500 B.C., legend and myth give place to fairly consistent and accurate records. It is beyond our scope here to record the rise and fall of China's twenty-one dynasties. Instead we will examine some of the highlights of Chinese history and the permanent influences which continue to shape it.

The Chou Dynasty (c. 1100 B.C.-200 B.C.) has been called by

political historians the "Age of Feudalism" in China. Although there were notable differences between Chinese "feudalism" and the feudalism of pre-Renaissance Europe, it is true that Chinese society was organized along "cellular," semi-feudal lines. The many small valleys of China were dominated by walled cities from which local overlords and their warrior bands both protected and exploited a local serflike farming population, while engaged in constant petty warfare among themselves. The Chou emperors, like the kings of feudal Europe, could not rule their domains directly, but depended upon the wavering allegiance of greater and lesser nobles—all of whom were masters within their own realms.

Cultural historians, on the other hand, have called the Chou period the Classical Age of Chinese history and have compared it with the Golden Age of Greece. For it was during Chou times that the philosophers Lao-tse, Confucius, and Mencius developed modes of thought and behavior which have dominated Chinese thinking down to the present day.

Lao-tse, who was born about 600 B.C., wrote a book of philosophy from which the religion of Taoism was derived. Basing itself largely upon ancient Chinese nature lore, Taoism ("The Way-ism") attempted to illustrate the natural road man must follow in order to achieve wisdom and holiness. Man's highest goal must be to escape from personal desire, which is only a painful illusion, by a mystical contemplation of himself and of nature. Perhaps because of its basis in nature-myth, Taoism over the centuries became a vast warehouse of miracles and magic. Very popular with the masses of uneducated Chinese peasants, Taoism degenerated into the worship of hundreds of local gods. A Taoist monastic system was established during the second century B.C., but Taoist monks soon devoted themselves to such evidences of human desire as an elixir of immortality and the legendary Alchemist's stone, which would transmute base metals into gold.

Confucius (551-479 B.C. ?) was both a philosopher of ethics and a busy public official. His teachings (he turned his home into a

"... Taoism degenerated into the worship of hundreds of local gods." Taoist temple of Ten Thousand Gods.

school for government officials and the sons of the aristocracy) have, for more than two thousand years, formed the moral basis and the ethical content of Chinese government and society. Living during times of warfare, rebellion, and tyranny, Confucius developed a system of morality and statecraft which was designed to bring about peace, justice, and universal order. The central conception of Confucianism was that of maintaining sympathy between men by maintaining right relationships among them. The Confucian Golden Rule may be stated as: "Treat those who are beneath you as you would be treated by those who are above you." Broadly speaking, therefore, the relationships between men are those of subordination. Women are subordinate to men, children are subordinate to their parents, the people are subordinate to the government, the government is subordinate to the emperor, and the emperor is subordinate to the will of heaven. But along with the concept of subordination goes that of responsibility. This is most dramatically illustrated by the role of the emperor. The emperor rules by a mandate from heaven—but he holds this mandate through his own good conduct. If the emperor is unjust or tyrannical, then heaven will withdraw its mandate and the people will have the right to overthrow the emperor, if they can. Thus any successful revolution would be self-justified by its very success. "Heaven decides as the people decide" is an ancient Chinese saying.

How was an emperor to act in order to maintain his mandate from heaven? Confucius said: "When a prince's personal conduct is correct, his government is effective without the issuing of orders. If his personal conduct is not correct, he may issue orders but they will not be followed." And just as the prince had a code of conduct proper to his station in life, each government official, from the highest to the lowest, had his own proper code of conduct. So intricate did the fathoming of these rules of conduct become that generations of Confucian scholars established themselves as an essential part of the Imperial government to advise it and maintain its morally correct nature—thus keeping the essential mandate from heaven.

The definition of just what constituted proper conduct and "right relationships" between people was the work not only of Confucius but of later scholars such as Mencius (371-288 B.C. ?), who, while adding to Confucianism a rigidity its founder may not have intended, also continued to emphasize the *responsibility* of the emperor to his subjects and their eventual right of rebellion against injustice and tyranny. Thus while Confucianism, in its insistence upon the eternal necessity of subordination among men, was perhaps the most effective system of thought ever devised for the maintaining of a conservative and aristocratic government, it also contained the moral basis of revolution.

The teachings of Confucius, which included many tales, bits of folklore, and poetry of ancient origin, as well as the commentaries written upon him, were gradually collected into a group of thirteen classics which were considered indispensable knowledge for any educated man. But in order to simplify this huge body of work (it runs to 120 volumes today), later scholars of the Sung Dynasty (A.D. 960-1279) selected four prime books, *The Analects [Sayings] of Confucius, The Book of Mencius, The Doctrine of the Mean [Middle Way]*, and *The Great Learning*, which were so brief and simple that any literate person could understand them. Although elements of superstition and even of magic gradually accumulated around Confucianism, it has never become a religion. Rather it is a code of human conduct sanctified by ancient usage.

In the second century B.C., one of China's feudal lords, the great conqueror Shih Huang Ti, built the first unified Chinese empire upon the wreckage of the semi-feudal Chou states. Although his work did not long survive his death, the Imperial system of government established by Huang Ti was to endure until 1911—more than two thousand years. Nor, after his death, did China ever again revert to a strictly semi-feudal political system of organization. A northerner himself, Huang Ti was alert to the continuing threat of barbarian invasion from the steppes of north-central Asia. To guard against it, he joined together various local structures into the Great Wall of China, which extended for more than fifteen hundred miles and was meant as a barrier against the warlike nomad tribes beyond. Like conquerors before and since, Huang Ti attempted to perpetuate his system by founding a dynasty of his heirs. But the Chin Dynasty lasted only a few decades, to be replaced by the Han. And the essential problems of Huang Ti's regime—the unification of China, defense against the nomad tribes of the north, and an orderly means of transferring power from one dynasty to another—remained to plague Chinese history. The problems are interlocking.

Wealth, power, and economic control in China depended on the ownership of land. In spite of a widespread commerce and a sizable

artisan class, China has always been an agricultural nation. The ownership of land and the grain in the landlord's warehouse have been the measure of his wealth. Also, the ability to levy and collect taxes on the produce of the land was the basis of state power until the Communist victory in 1949. The wealth of the Chinese land has, for many centuries, been itself based on the ability to irrigate vast regions around the Yellow and Yangtze rivers. But in spite of the skill of Chinese engineers, these and other Chinese rivers have a habit of overflowing their banks.

Between floods and taxes the Chinese peasant has always borne a crushing burden. In the sixteenth century the poet Chin Chu-yang wrote:

> At the fourth moon, the floods destroy our millet;
> At the fifth moon the floods destroy our corn.
> The corpses in the fields are many.
> No more millet, no more corn. But worse than all:
> The tax collector comes to give the death blow.

Of course both the state's taxes and the landlord's wealth rested on the backs of China's peasants. When the state was strong it could collect as much in taxes as it needed because it was able to prevent the landlords from siphoning off too much wealth in the form of exorbitant rents imposed on the peasants (and withheld subsequently from the tax rolls—the art or crime of tax evasion was perfected in China at an early date). Also, when the central government was weak, the landlords were able to hold the wealth of the land for themselves—thus further weakening the state. But the most important factor in this uneasy relationship was that the landlord and the tax collector were usually one and the same person!

In China, where agriculture depended upon irrigation to such a vast extent, the bookkeeping of land ownership was hugely complicated by the bookkeeping of water rights. As any American raised in southern California would understand, the ownership of water rights was often more important than the ownership of the land itself; and the calculations of just who was entitled to how much water at what times and at what rates was a tremendously intricate business. Only a well-educated man could keep the necessary records and make the necessary calculations. And to add to the difficulty of mastering the mathematics involved was the difficulty of becoming literate in one of the world's most complex languages.

A dictionary published A.D. 1716 under the Kang-hsi emperor contained no less than forty thousand separate characters, each standing for a different word. It has been estimated that while Chinese scholars may get along with seven or eight thousand characters, there are more than four hundred thousand potential in the Chinese complete vocabulary! Furthermore, it is even possible that the art of reading and writing Chinese was purposely kept as difficult as possible in order to preserve the "secret" of controlling the land and water rights upon which wealth was based. To acquire an education in so difficult a system of thought demanded much more leisure and wealth than most peasants could ever hope to enjoy. Thus, although there were instances of poor boys acquiring an education, generally it was the rich landlord who was competent to enter the government. So the landowning government official, the "literati" (literate man), was a self-perpetuating type. And as a government official, the wealthy landlord was most reluctant to impose taxes upon himself and his friends; he was much more inclined to simply add to the taxes taken directly from the peasants.

This process of heaping greater and greater burdens on the peasants' shoulders eventually and inevitably drove them to desperation —and rebellion. Time and again throughout Chinese history a seemingly settled, prosperous society would suddenly fall into chaos and revolution. Out of the endless peasant rebellions adventurers would arise who could organize the discontented masses for their own benefit, seizing state power, toppling the old dynasty, and eventually founding a new dynasty.

But once in power the new dynasty was faced by the same problems which had undermined the old. Wealth in China meant land; to tap that wealth in the form of taxes meant a large and intricately organized bureaucracy; bureaucracy meant the wealthy, educated landlord class; the government bureaucrat–wealthy landlord had conflicting interests, his own and the emperor's; when the emperor could no longer count on the active support of the "literati" and the passivity of the peasants, the cycle would repeat itself.

The fact that Chinese wealth was agricultural was also a basic factor in the relations between China and the warlike nomads

who roamed her northwestern frontier beyond Huang Ti's Great
Wall. Because these nomad tribes inhabited the dry plains of Mongolia, their conquest cost more than it was worth—the arid wastes
of their homelands were not good for farming and therefore useless
for tax purposes. Although successive Chinese dynasties sent out
expeditions beyond the Wall to break the military power of the
nomads, such military forays were usually indecisive and often
halfhearted. The nomads, being nomads, could simply strike their
tents and disappear with their flocks and herds into the vast distances
of central Asia—and when the Chinese armies withdrew, the nomad
horsemen would harass their retreat. Another means of keeping
peace along the northern frontiers was to encourage trade. This
trade was not entirely essential to the Chinese—they needed horses
and leather, but they were not searching for new markets in which
to dispose of surplus production. Instead they hoped that by allowing the nomad tribal chiefs to purchase what they wanted, they
could forestall plundering raids into China itself.

This habit of alternating war and trade with the northern barbarians led to the establishment of a convenient device for saving
both dignity and peace. The nomad tribes were allowed to send
missions into China which were politely called "embassies." These
"embassies" brought with them gold and fine horses and other products of their homelands, and this merchandise was called "tribute."
In return for their "tribute," they received from the Chinese
"presents" of silk and other Chinese products. Unfortunately, this
system had one important built-in fallacy. When the nomad tribesmen had seen for themselves the tremendous wealth of the Chinese
cities and land, their ambition was inevitably fired to conquer and
plunder; appeasement by way of trade, no matter what fine words
were used to describe it, worked no better for the Chinese against
the Mongolian tribes than it did for the Romans against the Ger-
manic tribes.

But on those occasions when the nomads gathered together sufficient strength to actually conquer China, they found themselves

enmeshed in the same problems which every new dynasty had to face. In order to tap the wealth of the land they had conquered, they needed the assistance of the vast "literati" bureaucracy—and they could only manage and manipulate this bureaucracy by themselves "going Chinese." Thus the nomad conquerors would find themselves submerged in the culture they sought to exploit; become just another dynasty in the long, long list of Chinese dynasties.

The Han Dynasty, which succeeded Huang Ti's short-lived Chin Dynasty, saw very important cultural developments in China. Of prime importance was the extending of education and the standardization of a Chinese written language. Another event of great cultural importance was the importation of Buddhism into China during the first century A.D. Already centuries old in India (its founder, Siddhartha Guatama, lived during the fifth century B.C.), Buddhism was brought to the Han domains by Indian missionaries. The new religion was not, at that time (before the decay of Taoist principles), very different from Taoism, since it taught that existence was desire, that desire meant suffering, and that suffering could only cease with an end to mortal existence. Furthermore, Buddhism offered an eight-fold "way" to escape from desire through right conduct and contemplation. Both Buddhism and Taoism, with their insistence on the undesirability of this life and an escape from it as the noblest course of human activity, were well suited to the fatalism of a people oppressed by a burdensome and apparently eternal hierarchy of exploitation.

The four-hundred-year-old Han Dynasty collapsed amid rebellions and chaos in A.D. 219—and succeeding periods of political disintegration, the establishment of new dynasties, their inevitable decay and fall, the occasional incursion of northern barbarians, only emphasized the continuing problems of the empire. During the sixth century A.D., with the establishment of the Sui Dynasty, northern China emerged as the most powerful region of the country. This was due to the fact that northern armies had to contend not only with southern Chinese kingdoms, but also with the frontier

nomads beyond the Great Wall. Thus northern soldiers learned cavalry tactics and the virtues of speedy and widespread strategic maneuvers, as well as the more formal tactics necessary to cope with rival kingdoms to the south. It was also during the Sui Dynasty that Chinese hydraulic engineering achieved its greatest triumph—the joining together of many regional canals into the Grand Canal, which linked the Yellow River and Yangtze River basins, thereby bringing flood control, irrigation, and improved communications to an area of many thousands of square miles.

The Tang Dynasty, established A.D. 618, was memorable for a rich flowering of Chinese art, commerce, and government administration. It was also during the Tang period that Buddhism, which had grown in wealth and power much as did the Catholic Church in medieval Europe, came into conflict with the central government. The Tang emperors waged a ruthless war against the Buddhist monasteries from which Chinese Buddhism never fully recovered. Although the religion survived as a cult, Confucianism remained the dominant Chinese ethical and moral philosophy.

While China alternated between long periods of settled rule and chaos, while northern Chinese kingdoms waged a continuing struggle against southern kingdoms, and dynasties rose and fell, the nomads beyond the Great Wall—the fierce Mongolian horsemen— waxed steadily stronger in population, organization, and the arts of war. Gathered together under the banners of Genghis Khan around A.D. 1200, the tremendous mass of Mongol tribesmen began that epic of conquest which earned them the name "Scourge of God" in Europe and founded the world's largest empire, stretching from the Pacific Ocean to the Danube River at its greatest extent. Genghis Khan himself only started the work of subduing China—his conquests were completed by his descendants until, by A.D. 1280, all of China lay in the Mongol grip.

". . . Buddhism offered an eight-fold 'way' to escape from desire through right conduct and contemplation."

Kublai Khan, grandson of Genghis, was the first Mongol emperor of all China; it was to his splendid court that Marco Polo found his way. And if the visit of the Polos to the court of the Great Khan was but a tiny event in the vast ocean of Chinese history, it was destined to have far-reaching repercussions. Yet the huge empire of the Khans, which Marco Polo described correctly as the greatest ever known, was doomed to fall barely one hundred years after his visit. However, the collapse of Mongol rule in China itself was unlike the collapse of any previous dynasty. For the Mongols, who had lived in close proximity to the Chinese Empire for untold centuries, were determined not to become Chinese. They well understood the dangers of submerging themselves in the conquered population. They tried to develop their own means of exploiting Chinese wealth—even to the extent of importing their own scholars and administrators from among the literate peoples of western Asia. Thus the Mongol regime remained, to the subject Chinese, not merely another exploitive dynasty—but a foreign one. And when, inevitably, the land taxes began to dry up and the peasants to rise in rebellion, the struggle against the Mongol Dynasty was tinged with a feeling new to the Chinese mentality—nationalism. For this was a direct struggle against a regime which had preserved its "foreign" character. And when a new dynasty—the Ming Dynasty—emerged triumphant to rule China in the middle of the fourteenth century, it was wreathed in nationalistic glory. Conquering Chinese armies not only swept the Mongols from China, but also pursued and defeated them in the wilds of Mongolia. Thereafter, although warfare continued intermittently against the Mongols, the tribes were steadily reduced in power. The Ming emperors determined to restore to China her cultural as well as her political integrity.

Yet—a little more than two hundred years later, the last Ming emperor, Chung Chen, found himself deserted and powerless as rebel armies from the south marched on the capital at Peking. For the Mings had failed to solve China's contradictory problems, as had every dynasty before them. It is related that Chung Chen, when he learned that his reign was at an end, climbed to the top of the hill known as Ching Shan on the outskirts of the Forbidden City. From there he could see the roofs and deserted courtyards of his palace—the Gate of Supreme Harmony, the Gate of Pure Limpidity, the Palace of Tranquility, and the wonderful gardens where grew the mysterious flower called the Flower of Silent Peace. Beyond Peking he could see clouds of yellow dust raised by the advancing rebel cavalry. The Empress, following her husband's wishes, had already taken poison. Emperor Chung Chen took a brush and traced a last message on the white silk cuff of his left sleeve: "We, poor in virtue and most contemptible of persons, have called down upon Our head the anger of the Gods. Our Ministers have deceived Us. We are filled with shame at the thought of meeting Our ancestors. We take from Our head the Imperial Crown and with Our hair falling about Our face We wait to be dismembered by the rebels. May they not make Our people suffer." Then the last Ming emperor hanged himself from the boughs of a nearby cedar tree.

But the rebel victory over the Ming Dynasty only paved the way for the accession to power of the Manchus, a coalition of semi-civilized northeastern tribes who substituted renewed foreign oppression for the decayed power of the Mings. Founded by a warrior-politician named Nurhachu, the Ching (Manchu) Dynasty drew its military strength from the frontier tribes, while its administrative strength was based on the allegiance of Chinese willing to collaborate with the new conquerors in return for the preservation of their own privileges. Much more politically sophisticated than the Mongols, the Manchus were able to exploit Chinese wealth without being submerged immediately by their newly conquered subjects. It was the Manchus who forced the Chinese to adopt the "pigtail" style of haircut to remind them of their subjection. And Manchu "Banners" (regiments) of seven or eight thousand men were stationed in many Chinese cities—retiring at night to fortresses known as "Manchu Cities" to preserve them from contaminating contact with the conquered population. In the civil service examinations, until the late eighteenth century, only the lower grades were open to Chinese, the more important posts being reserved to Manchu candidates. These Manchu administrators were known as *Man Ta-fin* (Manchu great man), later anglicized to "Mandarin." And to add insult to oppression, the Manchu emperors styled themselves as "protectors" and "preservers" of the old classical Chinese culture. By thus using the Chinese landlords and petty officials as tools with which to exploit the vast mass of the Chinese people, and at the same time preserving themselves at as great a distance as possible from the nation they ruled, the Manchus hoped to solve the problem of dominating and plundering the wealth of a culture infinitely higher and vaster than their own.

It is unlikely that the Manchu regime would have succeeded in maintaining its "foreign" character in the face of a continually growing Chinese nationalism which was never extinguished. But in any event the Manchus were themselves to fall victim to a means and morality of exploitation far more efficient and ruthless than anything they could imagine—the exploitation of China by nations of the Western world. For the time had come, after five thousand years of semi-isolation, for Chinese history to merge with the history of the rest of mankind. Of China's twenty-one dynasties, of the glory of the Imperial line which traced its mandate from heaven to the dawn of history, the Manchu Dynasty was to be the last. The dramatic collision of cultures which now ensued was to claim many more victims than the Manchu conquest and to influence profoundly the history of the world.

2

The Reluctant Dragon

THE PORTUGUESE and Spaniards were the first to arrive, followed soon after by the Dutch: merchant-adventurers sailing high-decked galleons, armed to the teeth, and determined to share in the enormous profits of what soon came to be called "the China trade." Vasco da Gama and Magellan had shown the way—around Cape Horn or around the Cape of Good Hope—to the fabulous riches of the Orient. And to the hardy merchants of the sixteenth century, the silks and spices and other rare products with which they returned were well worth the months-long (sometimes years-long) voyage to the Chinese coast. Trading European-manufactured products, and sometimes paying in gold, Western merchants were doing business at such Chinese ports as Amoy and Canton even before the fall of the Ming Dynasty. Among the items of European manufacture which they carried with them were cannons and Christian missionaries, both (in spite of the Chinese invention of gunpowder

35

many centuries before) curiosities at the court of the Son of Heaven.

While the cannon were found useful (they helped win a great victory over the Manchus just before the Ming Dynasty collapsed), the missionaries were merely tolerated as practitioners of another harmless cult among the many which flourished in the empire. And the first missionaries—Catholics—were quite willing to adapt themselves to the conservative customs of China and concentrate on the saving of souls rather than the reform of society. In any event, both the mercantile and the religious representatives of the West (with certain exceptions among the missionaries) were regarded, in the time-honored traditions of the Celestial Empire, as barbarians.

Compared with these earlier comers, the English, who began to supplant their rivals along the China coast in the eighteenth century, were a revolutionary force. Already masters of many seas and rulers of a vast empire of their own, the English were not accustomed to being treated as barbarians. Furthermore, the English missionaries were Protestants who brought their prejudices to bear not only on China's essentially nonreligious philosophies but also on the entire Chinese social system. The view of many (but not all) Protestant missionaries was that the Chinese, as "benighted heathen," were an inferior people. Everything strange to European eyes—from the Buddhist temples to the bound feet of Chinese women—was to be attributed to the fact that they did not believe in the Protestant God. Therefore, the individual Chinese convert to Protestantism often was expected to accept not only the Christian religion but a European outlook on life as the only road to salvation. The growth of Protestantism in China was, in fact, a subverting and eventually revolutionary force. That English merchants, who were usually interested only in profits, were well aware of the possibly disruptive influences of Protestantism is shown by the fact that the first English missionary to China, Robert Morrison, had to travel by way of America in order to outwit the efforts of the British East India Company to prevent his arrival in the Orient.

Under the pressure of their early industrial revolution, English merchants competed for markets in China as members of a semi-official, government-protected monopoly. In the seventeenth and eighteenth centuries, European trade was dominated by the theory of "mercantilism," which held that wealth was money, not goods. Therefore, mercantilist nations attempted to obtain gold by increasing exports, taxing imports, and ruthlessly exploiting their colonies. State control was, of course, a vital part of this policy. In practice, a group of merchants would form a company and then receive from their government (in return for a healthy share of the profits) a monopoly giving them the exclusive right to trade in some geographical region. Needless to say, the government involved was quick to supply military force to protect the operations of such semi-public companies. The English brand of mercantilist philosophy was one of the prime causes of the American Revolution, and the Chinese appreciated it no more than did the American colonies.

The British monopoly for trade with the Orient was the East India Company, whose activities were extended from India to China. The wealth earned by this giant commercial organization, which maintained its own fleet and its own standing armies (in India), provided much of the capital which gave England a head-start in carrying through the industrial revolution. And industrialization at home created new economic pressure groups who competed with the East India Company abroad. Central to European problems in the China trade was the notable fact that the Chinese, who considered their civilization infinitely superior to that of the West, really had very little to buy from Western merchants.

When the Earl of Macartney headed a British embassy to the Chinese (Manchu) Emperor in 1793, he was received as another barbarian bringing tribute to the Son of Heaven. In a letter to King George III, the Emperor remarked: "As your Ambassador can see for himself, we possess all things. I set no value on objects strange or ingenious, and have no use for your country's manufactures." Nor was the Imperial insistence upon the performance of the

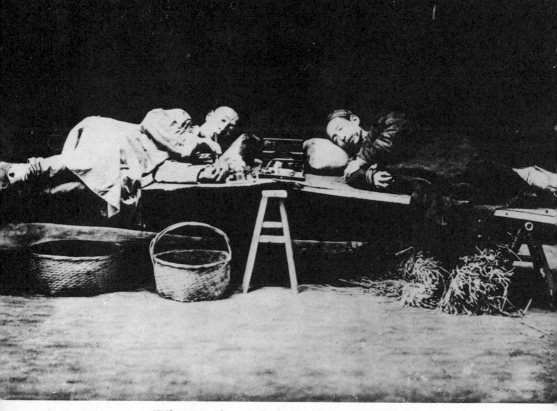

"The British, on the other hand, found that China was a good market for opium. . . ."

kowtow—kneeling three times and prostrating oneself nine times before the emperor—calculated to appeal to British sensibilities. (In fact in deference to the Earl of Macartney's dignity the ceremony was omitted.)

But if China needed little from the West, Western merchants needed much from China. How to pay for it? The Americans, who arrived in clipper ships from New England, solved the problem by bringing with them furs and ginseng root (valued as an aphrodisiac by the Chinese) from the Columbia River Indians and silver dollars from Mexico. The British, on the other hand, found that China was a good market for opium, which grew in India. Within a few years the Chinese began to consume so much of the new drug (eight thousand cases in 1824, thirty thousand cases in 1839) that English ships instead of bringing silver to China were sailing away from Canton with their holds full of silver. However, the introduction of the opium trade, with its profits huge enough to make bribery of government officials a profitable business, undermined the monopoly of the East India Company. Furthermore, the great increase in English manufacturing at home led the British government to insist that English ships bound for the Orient carry a certain percentage of manufactured goods even though the Chinese had so little use for them that they were sold at a loss.

The results of these changes in the China trade thoroughly alarmed the Chinese government. The clamor of English merchants for a greater and greater access to Chinese markets, their corruption of local Chinese officials, the loss of silver, and, above all, the terrible effects of opium upon those who smoked it, determined the Chinese to reduce foreign commerce and stamp out the opium trade completely. Long before 1839 the importation of opium into China had been forbidden by Imperial decree, and in that year Chinese officials at Canton burned large stocks of it illegally warehoused there. The governor of Canton, Lin Tsê-hsü (who was also an Imperial commissioner and member of the Emperor's war board), wrote a letter to Queen Victoria reprimanding her for allowing the opium trade to exist. "When your majesty receives this document," wrote Lin, "let us have a speedy communication in reply. . . . Do not evade or procrastinate. . . . We have heard that in your honorable barbarian country the people are not permitted to inhale the drug. If it is admittedly so deleterious how can profiting by exposing others to its malific power be reconciled with the decrees of heaven?" Nor did Commissioner Lin fail to remind the Queen of the humility she owed to the Emperor. "You, queen of your honorable barbarian nation, sit upon a throne occupied through successive generations by predecessors all of whom have been styled 'respectful' and 'obedient.' . . . Our celestial empire rules over ten thousand kingdoms. Most surely do we possess a measure of god-like majesty which ye cannot fathom. Still, we cannot bear to punish or exterminate without previous warning."

This was not the kind of letter that Queen Victoria was used to receiving from other monarchs—especially Asiatics. But Commissioner Lin was confident that English military power was much overrated. To the Emperor he reported: "Now here is why the people are dazzled by the name of England. Because her vessels are sturdy and her cannon fierce, they call her powerful. But the warships of the said barbarians are very heavy, taking water to the depth of tens of feet. . . . If we refrain from fighting with them on the sea, they have no opportunity to take advantage of their skill. Once in harbor these vessels become unwieldy." As for the British infantry—they lacked skill in using their swords and fists like proper soldiers. "Also, their legs are firmly bound with cloth and in consequence it is very inconvenient for them to stretch. Should they land it is apparent that they can do little harm. . . ."

But when the British infantry landed (at Tinghai) they soon demonstrated that their pants in no way impeded their agility, while their rifles and bayonets more than made up for whatever skill they may have lacked with swords and fists. Nor did the British fleet prove so unmaneuverable in coastal waters. After quickly sinking the Chinese fleet sent to oppose them, the English ships freely bombarded the coastal cities, the cruiser *Nemesis*, in spite of her deep draft, sailing up the Yangtze River to knock out the coastal forts. The unequal struggle ended with the Treaty of Nanking in 1842. In this treaty, and in subsequent negotiations, the Chinese were forced to pay for the opium they had burned as well as for the cost of the war.

In 1853, as a result of disorders in Shanghai, a maritime customs service, staffed by English and French officials, was established in China's ports. Tariff treaties placed so low a tax upon imports into China (five per cent) that the empire was thrown open to a flood of Western-manufactured items which prevented the growth of native Chinese industry. And, whereas the Chinese had formerly limited Western traders to the single port of Canton, the Treaty of Nanking opened several other coastal cities to foreign commerce.

Gradually these cities became known as the Treaty Ports—and one of them, Hong Kong, eventually was ceded outright to the British Crown. Within the Treaty Ports, such as Shanghai and Amoy, the right of Westerners to live in their own separate settlements was recognized. Within these "international settlements" Chinese law did not prevail. Instead foreign consuls had jurisdiction over their own nationals, and any Chinese who brought a civil suit against a foreigner had to have it judged under foreign law. In still another treaty (signed in 1843), the English were able to establish the "most favored nation" principle, which meant that any privilege won from the Chinese by any foreign country could be equally enjoyed by all foreign countries. The United States was the first nation to take advantage of this provision by a treaty in 1844.

But if foreign merchants and their gunboats posed a threat to the continued independence of the Celestial Empire, a much graver, if less apparent, danger was the steady subversion of Confucian ideas by foreign missionaries when combined with the continuing misery of peasant life. For decades, an increasing number of them had gone out into the countryside to preach the doctrines of Christ. And if the Chinese peasants remained skeptical about the more mystical aspects of Christianity, they welcomed certain parts of Christian doctrine. Christianity, it will be recalled, was originally a very revolutionary body of thought when first preached to the subjects of the Roman Empire. It was equally revolutionary when expounded to the downtrodden peasants of Imperial China. In 1850, the semiconverted peasant masses of southern China erupted into one of the largest and bloodiest rebellions in world history.

The Taiping (Heavenly Kingdom) Rebellion was not, of course, motivated only by Christian doctrine. Basically it was a peasant revolt against starvation (there were drought and widespread famine in the years 1846-1848), the age-old oppression of the tax collector and the landlord, and the new "foreign" oppression of the Manchu Dynasty—a dynasty which had shown its weakness in being unable to cope with the barbarian Westerners. It was led by a disappointed scholar named Hung Hsiu-chuan, one of the most re-markable men in Chinese history.

Hung Hsiu-chuan was born in 1812 in southern China. As a young man he tried three times to pass the civil service examinations held annually in the city of Canton. Three times he failed. At the time of his third failure he fell ill, and in delirium he believed he saw a venerable old man who commanded him to save humanity. When he recovered from this attack he returned to his native village to become a country schoolmaster—and with him from Canton he brought a Western Christian religious tract in Chinese entitled: *Good Words Exhorting the Age.* Hung did not get around to reading this pamphlet for six years, but when he did and when he had digested its biblical quotations, the country schoolmaster was convinced that the old man who had appeared to him at Canton was none other than God himself—the Christian God.

Hung soon returned to Canton to spend two months learning Christianity at the house of Reverend Issachar J. Roberts, a Protestant missionary. When once again he returned to his native village, he was, nominally, a Christian. He soon gathered followers who made a practice of destroying the idols in local temples and who, when Hung was forced to give up his schoolteaching by the outraged local landlords, followed him into the hills. There they were joined by peasant refugees from unsuccessful local uprisings. Hung's preaching soon took on an anti-Manchu tinge, and in 1851, his movement gave itself the name of *Taiping tien-kue*, or Heavenly Kingdom of Great Peace, thereby raising the standard of open rebellion against the Manchus.

Once launched, the rebellion rapidly gained strength: soon much of southern China lay within the Taiping power. At the beginning of 1853, rebel armies captured and burned the great city of Hankow in their advance up the Yangtze valley. In March of 1853 the rebels captured Nanking and established it as the Taiping capital. Manchu armies could not withstand the ferocity of the Taiping assault and it seemed inevitable that the Manchu Dynasty must fall. It was saved partly by internal contradictions within the Taiping movement and partly by the intervention of the Western powers.

Taiping Christianity was peculiarly adapted by Hung Hsiu-chuan to serve the purposes of his peasant uprising. The Christian God adopted by Hung was really the Old Testament God—an avenger and destroyer of the unfaithful. He was also an ever-present God who spoke directly not only to Hung but also to Hung's two chief lieutenants. Markedly absent from the Taiping doctrine were the Christian conceptions of humility, love for neighbors, and forgiveness. Perhaps of greater importance within the rebel movement were Taiping conceptions of land ownership. Hung and his followers preached a primitive type of communism whereby land was to be redistributed—taken from the rich landlords and given to peasant families who would not own it, but work it together and divide its produce equally among themselves—much as a Soviet collective farm works today. During the years of bloody warfare of the Taiping Rebellion, these conceptions were never put into actual practice—but the preaching of land redistribution was perhaps the most powerful factor in gathering the peasant millions behind Taiping banners.

At first many Westerners resident in China welcomed the Taiping movement. It was avowedly a Christian movement and its purpose—to overthrow the corrupt and anti-Western Manchu Dynasty—seemed to fit in with Western policy. But it was not long before Western merchants and missionaries realized that the Taipings were attempting nothing less than the rebirth of a strong and independent China and preaching doctrines of self-reliance, personal liberty, and communal effort which would completely undermine the Western commercial interest in exploiting the Chinese Empire. The corrupt Manchu regime could at least be bribed, threatened, and in other ways controlled to Western advantage—the Taipings could not.

Perhaps more deadly to Taiping hopes than the growing Western opposition was the fear which the rebels inspired in the land-lord-gentry class. Although Chinese scholar-administrator-landlords were subject to the Manchus, they found themselves much more dangerously threatened by Taiping doctrines than by Manchu overlordship. For in their preaching of economic equality, of social equality between men and women and against such ancient customs as arranged marriages, slavery, cruel tortures and punishments, and the use of opium—in short, against the inherited mode of behavior—the Taipings were threatening the very structure of Chinese society and the basis of landlord and scholar-administrator existence. Therefore the educated governmental classes of China quickly sided with the Manchu Dynasty in its struggle, thereby depriving the rebel movement of a necessary intellectual leadership.

From their new capital at Nanking, the Taiping armies launched a "great northern expedition" against the Imperial stronghold of Peking in 1853. But even as their armies came to within thirty miles of the Imperial capital, the tide of rebellion was beginning to recede. The Western powers, now thoroughly alarmed by Taiping successes, first decided to prevent their entry into the Treaty Ports. This was soon followed by open clashes between Western and Taiping forces and by Western collaboration with the Manchus. An American soldier of fortune, Frederick Townsend Ward of Salem, Massachusetts, was placed in command of one of the Manchu armies, styled the "Ever Victorious Army." When Ward was killed, command of this force of mixed Chinese and foreign mercenary troops passed to the English General Charles George "Chinese" Gordon. Thereafter, the Manchu regime pressed the rebel forces with almost continuous attack, slowly driving them back to the south. Hung Hsiu-chuan, the "Heavenly King," committed suicide, and on July 19, 1864, Manchu forces recaptured the Taiping capital of Nanking. Thousands of rebels were massacred by the victorious Imperial troops—but few surrendered. By the end of the Taiping revolt, in 1864, much of the Celestial Empire had been ravaged and an estimated ten million people killed. But the scholar-landlord class had saved its privileges, the Manchu Dynasty had saved its decadent regime, and the Western powers had saved their commercial exploitation of China. The ultimate casualties in this pyrrhic victory were any hope of Christianizing China and any hope of developing a reasonable life under democratic auspices for the Chinese people.

By relying upon the Western powers to help it crush the Taipings, the Manchu Dynasty had placed itself in a position of greater and greater dependence upon British, French, and other foreign interests. From now on the Westerners would press their demands ruthlessly. Thus when, in 1858, the Emperor delayed in signing over more rights to Western merchants in the Treaty Ports, the British and French dispatched a punitive expedition under Lord Elgin. Lord Elgin, whose father had already become famous for his looting of the Greek Parthenon, kept a diary in which he tried (unsuccessfully) to pacify his conscience in the face of his duties. "I thought," he wrote, "with bitterness of those who for the most selfish motives are trampling on this antique civilization. There is a certain word 'loot' which unfortunately gives a venial meaning to what should be called, in good English, robbery."

While Lord Elgin's soldiers looted and burned the priceless Summer Palace in Peking, a French observer, Count d'Herisson, observing French troops in action, wrote: "I saw troopers with their heads stuck in the Empress' red lacquer coffers; others buried in piles of brocades and lengths of silk, yet others pocketing rubies, sapphires, pearls and pieces of rock crystal. . . . The sappers had brought their axes and broke up the furniture to prise out the precious stones with which it was inlaid. One of them was gravely hammering at an enchanting Louis XV clock to obtain the dial, on which the hours were marked in figures of crystal. He took them for diamonds."

Among the privileges that this example of Western savagery wrung from the hapless Manchus was that of preaching Christianity freely. The pertinent treaty article read: "The principle of the Christian religion . . . 'do unto others as you would they should do unto you' constitutes a highly laudable morality. In consequence those who preach these doctrines in a spirit of peace shall not be vexed or persecuted as a result of their beliefs." As the Chinese negotiators signed this treaty they could see the ruins of the summer palace still smoking in the distance.

In the years that followed, the Western impact on China gathered increasing force and momentum. No longer content to rule over their independent enclaves in the Treaty Ports, European imperialist powers now dispatched their gunboats up Chinese rivers to control trade deep inside the country. And as the Westerners closed in on the empire by sea, so tsarist Russia advanced overland. During the latter half of the nineteenth century the Russians secured (by the convention of Peking in 1860) control over the entire coast of Manchuria to the Korean border. Later, when the trans-Siberian railroad was completed in 1895, Russia secured the right to administer connecting rail lines through Chinese Manchuria. In 1898 the cities of Port Arthur and Dairen were "leased" to Russia. And in central Asia, Russian troops first infiltrated and then seized large areas of Chinese Turkestan. The tsar's government continued its policy of encroachment up to the very eve of the Russian Revolution. In 1911, at Russian instigation, Outer Mongolia proclaimed itself independent of the Chinese Empire and, in 1915, became a Russian protectorate in all but name.

Nor were England and France to be left behind in the race for Chinese spoils. In the 1880's Britain began that long infiltration of Tibet which resulted in the capture of Lhasa in 1904 and the flight of the Dalai Lama, while France proceeded to annex the lands which became French Indo-China. Tibet had been under Chinese rule and Indo-China had been a tributary state for many centuries. If such outlying regions of the empire could be seized, why-not divide up China itself into colonies? With the entry of Imperial Germany and a modernized Japan upon the imperialist scene, it seemed certain that China would suffer the fate of Africa. While the German Empire grabbed its share of China in the Shantung peninsula, Japan, a close neighbor, posed a deeper threat.

For thousands of years the Chinese had considered Japan as merely an insignificant barbarian land. The common Chinese term for the Japanese was "dwarf slaves." There had been a few clashes over the centuries between Chinese and Japanese fleets—battles usually won by China. Japan's culture, her religion, her very language had been in large part derived and in every way mightily influenced by Chinese sources. Like China, Japan had maintained a "splendid isolation" from the rest of the world, and, like China, Japan had been more or less forcefully opened to Western commerce by Western fleets. But the response of the Japanese to the events which followed Commodore Matthew Perry's visit in 1853-1854 was markedly different from China's reaction to Western influences. The Japanese hastened to copy the superior mechanics, organization, and scientific learning of the West, rebuilding their national life with such thoroughness that within fifty years they possessed formidable modern armies and fleets—and an expanding and hungry industrial complex. Eager to win the same trade privileges within the crumbling Chinese Empire as the Western powers, Japan declared war on China in 1894—ostensibly to secure independence from Chinese overlordship for Korea. To the surprise of the Chinese and of most of the rest of the world, Japan's modern fleets and regiments were quickly successful. In 1895, by the treaty of Shimonoseki, China was forced to give up her claims to sovereignty in Korea (which quickly became a Japanese puppet state) and to cede to Japan Formosa, the Pescadores Islands, and the Liaotung Peninsula.

The final dismemberment of China was deferred temporarily at least partly by the so-called Open Door policy enunciated by American Secretary of State John Hay in 1899. In a series of notes to the European powers and Japan, supported by the British Foreign Office, Secretary Hay proposed that no matter what any one nation took for itself in China, it must leave an "open door" to American trade and commerce. The Open Door policy did not suggest that imperialist demands on China should cease—it merely registered a "me too!" claim on the spoils. But perhaps of more importance in preventing the final cannibalization of the Celestial Empire was the fierce competition which developed between the imperialistic powers over their "rights" and "spheres of influence" in Asia. As rivalry for the markets of China became intense, European powers began to realize that a clash between them at Shanghai or Tientsin might very well lead to war in Europe itself—an eventuality they were unwilling to risk at the moment. An example of what too much greed in the Orient could lead to was the Russo-Japanese war of 1905 in which Japan quickly defeated Russian armies in Manchuria and sank Russian fleets in the China Sea. Not only was the war fought over who should have control of Manchuria—a Chinese province—but it was fought entirely upon Chinese soil!

The Manchu Dynasty and Chinese political leaders made various attempts during the decades between 1860 and 1900 to ward off foreign penetration and domination of their country—but few were successful. Nearly all were undermined by the determination of the Chinese landlord and administrative classes to retain their privileges at whatever cost. These privileges were based on Confucianism as a way of life and absolutism as a way of government. But neither concept could be maintained in the face of the Western invaders. For to protect themselves from Western aggression the Chinese would have to adopt Western science, technology, arms, and organization. However, these instruments could not be used to preserve ancient Confucian values. Gunboats and factories bring their own philosophy with them.

An example of the fruitless Chinese attempt to imitate Western technocracy without adopting Western values was the "self-strengthening movement" of the 1860's and 1880's. Originating among those Chinese officials who had to deal directly with Westerners in the Treaty Ports, it soon spread to certain liberal circles in Peking and throughout the provinces. But the attempts of lower echelon administrators to copy Western methods were constantly undermined by the upper strata of officialdom. The establishment of an interpreters' college in Peking at which young diplomats were to be trained to deal with Western negotiators had to be defended against the attacks of scholars on the false ground that "Western sciences borrowed their roots from ancient Chinese mathematics. Westerners still regard their mathematics as coming from the Orient. . . . China invented the method, Westerners adopted it."

The jealousy with which the landlord-administrator class defended its ancient usages may be illustrated by the fate of Yung Wing. Taken by missionaries to the United States in 1847, Yung Wing was graduated from Yale University in 1854. But when he returned to China he had to wait ten years before his knowledge of the West was put to use—and then he found himself only a minor administrator-interpreter. When Yung Wing proposed that other Chinese be sent abroad to study he had to wait fifteen years to get any action on his proposal. Finally, in 1872, Yung Wing led a group of young Chinese scholars, dressed in their traditional long gowns, to New Haven, Connecticut. With them came old-style Chinese teachers who were to instruct them in Confucian doctrine and also a teacher who was specially appointed to make certain that the youngsters were not corrupted by Western morals. The entire project had to be given up after ten years.

The bedrock of opposition to change was, of course, the Manchu Dynasty. In 1862 a new emperor had to come to the Celestial throne, Tung Chih. But since Tung Chih was still a child, his mother, Tzu Hsi, was appointed Empress Regent to act for him. Resolute, cunning, cruel, and tyrannical, Tzu Hsi presided over one of the most corrupt and decadent courts known to history. She regarded China as her private estate—the "Hatamen Octroi" tax on all merchandise entering the city of Peking was devoted largely to buying the old lady's cosmetics. During her regency, she managed to lay hands on a huge fund which had been laboriously raised through taxes to build a new Chinese navy and spent most of it on a new summer

Empress Dowager

palace at Peking to replace the one burned by Anglo-French forces in 1860. In the middle of the lake on the palace grounds she caused a marble boat to be built on pilings—and this was one of the few ships China ever got for her naval taxes. The Empress Regent used it as a pavilion on which to drink tea at sunset. When her son died in 1875, the Empress Dowager immediately found another child to take his place so that she could continue to act as Regent. The new Emperor, Kuang Hsü, was as much dominated by the Dowager as her own son had been. Although this fierce old lady retired when Kuang Hsü came of age in 1889, she was to be heard from again.

The shock of defeat by Japan in 1895 led to yet another convulsive effort to reform Chinese society. Led by a fiery Cantonese scholar named Kang Yu-wei, the reformers of 1898 advocated the establishment of a limited constitutionalism, modernization of government administration, and a general "Westernization" of Chinese institutions. Kang shocked conservative scholars (who demanded his head for such audacity) by publishing a work entitled *Confucius as a Reformer* in which he tried to picture Confucius as standing for the rights of the people against unjust rulers. But so persuasive were the words of Kang Yu-wei and his followers that they attracted the attention and support of the Emperor, Kuang Hsü. During a hundred-day period in the summer of 1898, the Emperor, on the advice of Kang Yu-wei, issued a cataclysmic series of decrees intended to reform Chinese society from top to bottom. The proclamations, which had the force of instant law, dealt with government administration, the civil service examinations, agriculture, medicine, the armed forces, the penal code, the police, postal services, commerce, and even with study abroad.

The Hundred Days of Emperor Kuang Hsü produced real consternation among the officials of the empire. Landlords, administrators, scholars—many saw themselves threatened by the reform decrees. They turned to the old Empress Dowager, Tzu Hsi, and, with support from the military, deposed the young Emperor and declared the old lady once more Empress Regent. The Emperor was imprisoned in the Imperial Palace at Peking, his decrees were immediately declared null and void, some of the reformers were beheaded, and Kang Yu-wei himself was forced to flee to Japan. If it had not been clear before, it was now self-evident that Chinese modernization could come only through revolutionary activity.

Traditionally, Chinese revolutionary activity had often been channeled through secret societies. Many of these, such as the White Lotus Society, numbered thousands of members. The White Lotus Society dated back to the Mongol Dynasty and had religious (Buddhist) overtones. Like other secret societies it had its secret handclasps and passwords and membership lists and rituals. But unlike certain Western secret societies, the Chinese groups had a real reason for their mumbo jumbo: the constant threat of exposure to and massacre by the Imperial authorities. With the advent of the Manchu regime, such societies as the White Lotus devoted themselves to the overthrow of the foreign dynasty. In 1796 the White Lotus Society placed itself at the head of a widespread peasant rebellion against landlords and Manchus that was put down only after five years of costly civil war. Although the Taiping rebels held themselves aloof from the powerful Triad Society, which had inherited the White Lotus tradition, Chinese secret societies gained in strength throughout the nineteenth century and organized more than a few local rebellions against the Manchus. And, as it became more and more apparent that the Manchus continued in power only on the sufferance of the Western powers who plundered the country, the secret societies soon adopted an anti-Western policy. The climax of this disorganized but profound hatred of both the Manchu Dynasty and the oppressive imperialism of the West came in 1900 with the Boxer Rebellion.

The Boxers were a secret society similar to the White Lotus and Triad societies. Their proper name was *I Ho Chuan,* or Righteous Harmony Bands, their nickname deriving from the emphasis they placed on the art of boxing for exercise and self-defense. Raising the standard of rebellion against both the Manchus and the Western powers, the Boxer Rebellion, though suppressed in south China, soon seized control of the countryside in the north and marched on Peking. The Empress Dowager, Tzu Hsi, recognizing a real threat to the Manchu Dynasty, cleverly decided to side with the rebels. Manchu officials thought that the Western powers would make a convenient lightning rod to divert Boxer wrath from themselves. More than two hundred Christian missionaries were killed by the Boxers in north China, and for two months during the summer of 1900, the foreign embassies in the legation compound at Peking were besieged. Yet the Boxer attacks were never really

"More than two hundred Christian missionaries were killed by the Boxers in north China. . . ." Missionaries pray at the site of a tomb for their brethren slaughtered outside Peking.

pushed home because the higher Manchu officials realized that to attack Westerners was suicidal in the long run.

The European governments and the United States hastened to dispatch expeditionary forces to relieve the Peking legations. Kaiser Wilhelm II of Germany, seeing his troops off for China, advised them to comport themselves "like Huns." They were to show no mercy to the wretched Chinese. The Kaiser's advice was hardly necessary but it created a label which was to stick to German armies in later wars.

Once again foreign troops went on an orgy of killing and destruction in the Celestial Empire. Pierre Loti, writer, journalist, member of the *Académie française,* described the activities of French colonial troops in Peking: "Everything has been sacked, torn and destroyed . . . and here and there, legs, hands, heads and bundles of hair. . . . One should see the eagerness with which our soldiers fling everything outside, hear their gay laughter. In the bright midday sun the courtyard [of the Imperial Palace at Peking] is soon a shambles. . . ." As for the Chinese, Loti parroted the old nonsense about "four or five hundred millions of brains diametrically opposed to ours, brains we shall never be able to decipher."

Of course the Chinese were made to pay for the Boxer Rebellion by the victorious Westerners—over 330,000,000 dollars. And although the United States, in a belated attack of conscience, offered to use its share of the Boxer indemnity to pay for the education of young Chinese in the United States, American commercial interests, like those of the European powers, hastened to gather the fruits of new impositions and preferences in the creaking empire.

The Empress Dowager, who now pretended (unsuccessfully) to the Westerners that she had all along been against the Boxer Rebellion, returned to Peking in 1902, finally realizing that some sort of reform was indispensable if her dynasty was not to topple. But how gradual this reform was to be was indicated by an Imperial pronouncement in 1907 which threatened people who were too impatient. "Among the people, the merchants, the 'literati' and even the notables," the Empress observed, "there are ignorant creatures who, under the pretext of working for the establishment of constitutional laws, band together to busy themselves with public and foreign policies, thus provoking great disorder and propagating evil doctrines harmful to the country. . . . If in future men try to raise the people we shall punish them in the severest possible manner."

But reformist ideals, Imperial decrees, all were hopelessly inadequate now. History had left both reformers and Manchus behind. Two generations of Chinese, exposed to wider and wider contact with Western thought, had grown up since the Opium War. Experience had taught them that only fundamental and nationwide revolution could begin to solve China's problems. And behind them were vast millions of impoverished peasants and exploited city workers whose misery had only been multiplied by the Western invasion of the Celestial Empire. It was these millions—long suffering and long voiceless—who were to reshape China's destiny in the decades ahead. In order to understand the passion of their struggle and the paths it took, it would be well to take a closer look at both the myth and the reality of the life of the average man in China—a life which was on the threshold of dramatic change.

3

The Life and Times
of "Old Hundred Names"

EVEN BY his nickname the average Chinese is reminded of his long history, his deep roots in the land. In Chinese the equivalent of "Mr. Everybody," or "John Doe," is *Lao Pai Hsing*—Old Hundred Names. The names referred to are those of the legendary one hundred families who (mythically) founded China many thousands of years ago. Far from being one of a nameless crowd, the average man in China is accorded the dignity of an aristocratic ancestry. But until very recently, that was all the dignity he could claim. His actual position in the scheme of the Celestial Empire is expressed

by one of the most ancient of Chinese Poems, "The Hundred Names":

> *From dawn to dusk*
> *I sweat and till*
> *my meager field.*
>
> *I dig a well*
> *and sow my corn,*
> *I eat my rice*
> *And drink my wine.*
>
> *What harm then*
> *Can the Governor do me?*
> *If there be no war*
> *I can go on living.*

For to "go on living" was often the highest aspiration of Old Hundred Names. He had been born into a society of rigid relationships, defined not only by Confucian doctrines, but also by hard economic necessity. Caught between the oppression of the landlord and the landlord-dominated government (of whatever dynasty), he had little enough time to partake in the rich cultural traditions of art and learning which were the prerogatives of the rich. His life, somewhat like that of a European serf of the Middle Ages, was centered exclusively around his family and his village, which was but a collection of families, usually interrelated. When the world outside his village touched Old Hundred Names it was usually a disaster—the depredations of local bandits, the brutal press gangs of one army or another, the calculated robbery of the tax collector, and, later, the savagery of the colonial troops of some Western nation. The rhythm of his life was measured in the procession of the planting and harvesting seasons, punctuated by famines, pestilences, and wars, and underscored by the everlasting bondage of debt.

Because of the constant exploitation of his labor, Old Hundred Names never had the chance to get together enough capital (or land) to either mechanize agriculture or use large-scale methods. Throughout the Yangtze valley (and, in fact, throughout Southeast Asia) the rice crop is transplanted, seedling by seedling, from its seed beds to the rice paddies (terraces in the hills, irrigated and ankle-deep in water) by hand—endless rows of peasants walking backwards, bending at the waist, in the greatest expenditure of pure muscle power in the world. When the rice is mature the fields are drained and the crop harvested—again by hand. Yet, given enough hands and enough water, there is probably no way by which a greater yield per acre could be obtained. An American farmer, using the world's most advanced methods, may harvest twenty-five bushels of wheat per acre; the Chinese farmer and his family will glean forty-two bushels of rice per acre. But it takes the American farmer only one and a half man-days to harvest his bushels, while Old Hundred Names will spend twenty-six man-days harvesting his.

When his long labor in the fields was ended by sunset, Old Hundred Names returned to a small house made of sun-dried bricks or bamboo with a dirt floor, sometimes an oil lamp, and paper for windows. At least half, usually two-thirds, of his income went to buy food; what little was left over was for everything else from clothes to rent. His house generally had about four room-sections for each three inhabitants and it was not unusual for the entire family to sleep on the same brick bed. Old Hundred Names rarely tasted meat and his hands rarely knew the feel of iron. His plow was made of wood. His life expectancy was not more than twenty-six years and his chances of spending those years victimized by malnutrition or some crippling disease were frighteningly high.

Living under such crowded conditions, and always on the brink of outright starvation, Old Hundred Names developed a social code of behavior based on order—order in all things. Reinforced by the teachings of Confucianism, this social code made the family, not the individual, the basic social unit. Within the family the father

". . . this social code made the family, not the individual, the basic social unit."

was an absolute autocrat. His wish was law and he could go so far as to sell his children into bondage if he wished. Naturally he controlled all the meager wealth of the family, arranged the marriages of his children (often at the age of eight or earlier), took concubines if he could afford them, dismissed his wife if she displeased him, and received the veneration of his sons in this life and the next. As part of the ritual of authority built up over the centuries, Old Hundred Names would scrupulously set aside certain days each year on which the memory of his ancestors would be celebrated by burning paper money on the family altar and offering up incense, rice cakes, and whatever else his small resources allowed.

But if Old Hundred Names's life was a hard one, it was nothing compared to the misery he might have known had he been born a girl. In that case he would have been lucky not to have been killed

in infancy. The birth of a girl to a Chinese peasant family was something of a disaster. Here was another mouth to feed—and a creature to raise who would not bring in any income through her labor. Unable to work in the fields, a girl could be expected only to help with the housework. An old proverb hinting at infanticide, "If the river could speak, the trees on the river bank would weep tears of blood," reminds Old Hundred Names of the fate of generations of girl infants. Nor was a girl always lucky to escape death in infancy. As a child her feet were tightly bound in cloth to prevent their growing—and her wandering very far from the family hut. She was probably already married by the time she was twelve—a marriage arranged by the village astrologer-soothsayer in accordance with the dictates of the stars. And when she married, she married an entire family, a clan, rather than simply a husband. She would be a household slave to her mother-in-law and her new relatives until she too became a mother-in-law. More than sixteen hundred years ago, the poet Fu Hsuan wrote:

> *It is sad to be born in the body of a girl,*
> *Nothing on earth is of so little account.*
> *No one rejoices when a girl is born,*
> *She brings nothing to the hearth.*
>
> *As she grows up she hides in her room;*
> *She is afraid to be seen by men.*
> *No tears are shed when she leaves the house,*
> *But her own tears flow like the spring rain.*

Old Hundred Names might never have seen his wife until the day she arrived at his family's house, for he had as little say in the matter of whom he would marry as she did. The personal tragedies

"She was probably already married by the time she was twelve. . . . She would be a household slave to her mother-in-law. . . ."

which arose from these customs have been celebrated in Chinese literature and drama for two thousand years. Nor was the tragedy always individual. For by custom the bride's family had to give her a dowry and had to pay for the marriage feast—an expense which often meant the absolute ruin of a peasant family. Since divorce was out of the question for a woman, if the bride was too savagely mistreated in her new home, her only escape was through suicide. If that occurred, then her former family had the right to sue her in-laws—and the suit would be ruinous to both families.

Of course Chinese legend also has it heroines—clever or beautiful women who managed to circumvent their status in one way or another, and happiness did sometimes come through prearranged marriages. But these are tales of the exceptional.

And if Old Hundred Names could expect little joy from his family, he was almost certain of catastrophe at the hands of nature. His lands, as we have seen, depended almost entirely upon irrigation for their fertility. But the great rivers were uncontrolled. For more than two thousand years the Yellow River has overflowed its banks on an average of once every two and one-half years; the river Hwai, north of the Yangtze, has flooded every second year for more than seventy generations. Chinese chronicles record more than 979 floods between 246 B.C. and A.D. 1948. During the floods of 1931, the mighty Yangtze River flooded eight provinces, ruining seven million acres of land and drowning or driving from their homes more than fifty million people. How even these disasters were used by the landlords to exploit their peasants is illustrated by the play entitled *The Bride of the River God*, an ancient tragedy set in the fourth century B.C.

The play deals with the people of a tiny village—Yeh Tu—who are poor and wretched because the river overflows its banks every year, swallowing their harvests and destroying their homes. The rich landlords and their friends, the village priests, have found a remedy for these evils by building a huge and expensive temple in which the River God is worshipped. The peasants bring their offerings to the temple—grain and pork and wine—and the priests, of course, take their share. But even this does not appease the hunger of the River God. The priests announce that the River God requires each year the sacrifice of the village's most beautiful young girl, who is to be placed on a raft, her hair adorned with flowers, and left to the rushing current of the waters. This custom affords the priests with another means of graft. For by paying a large sum, the village's richer peasants can persuade them to choose someone else's daughter for the great honor of meeting the River God.

But a new governor has been appointed to rule the village. This man, Hsi-men Pao, is as clever as he is honest and fearless. He announces that this year he will himself preside at the ceremony of the river sacrifice. But at the last moment before the tearful young girl is to be set afloat on her raft he stands up.

"That bride is not beautiful enough for the mighty River God," he declares. "Let the high priest himself go to question the God, to know which of our maidens he would choose to have."

And the good governor and his guards fling the high priest into the waters. Since the high priest does not return with the River God's reply, the governor proceeds to fling each of the temple priests in turn into the river after him. When these do not return, he flings all the rich landlords of the village after them. Then the governor goes himself to the temple of the River God to ask what the God really wants. When he emerges he has the answer—what the River God truly desires is that the peasants should dig twelve canals to divert the waters of the river from their village and fields.

This play, twenty-three centuries old, is still one of the most popular in China. As the priests and landlords are thrown into the river, the audience shouts: *"Hao! Hao!"* (very good!) But it will be noticed that Governor Hsi-men Pao has to proceed very cautiously

NEXT PAGES: *"This play, twenty-three centuries old, is still one of the most popular in China."*

and cleverly and pretend always that what he does is the will of heaven. For after thousands of years of oppression, Old Hundred Names had come to believe that his woes were divinely inspired. This fatalism—the feeling that no human effort can avert the calamitous will of heaven—has often been confused with the fatalistic pose of the Chinese scholar-gentry who imbibed resignation not from necessity but from the teachings of Confucius.

As recently as twenty years ago, the landlords and scholars of Old Hundred Names's village were accustomed to beginning their letters to each other with the salutation: "Dear Mr. Underfoot—" This was because seven hundred years before Christ, one of the Emperor's best friends, out of love of his ruler, had allowed himself to die by embracing a flaming tree. The Emperor had the tree cut down and made himself a pair of sandals from its wood. He wore these sandals every day and when he thought of his friend murmured sadly: "Underfoot, underfoot." For the following thirteen centuries the expression "underfoot" meant great friendship.

There are a thousand and one fables intended to illustrate the passive acceptance of fate by Old Hundred Names; for example, the Fable of the Lost Horse:

Once upon a time there was a poor old peasant who lived in the northwest, near the barbarian lands. One day he lost his only horse. But when his neighbors came to offer condolences he said: "How can you be sure it wasn't really a piece of good luck?" A few weeks later the old peasant's horse returned, accompanied by a fine thoroughbred of barbarian stock. But when the old peasant's friends came to congratulate him, he said: "How can you be sure this isn't a piece of bad luck?" Sure enough, a few days later, the peasant's son fell from the new horse and broke his leg. Once again the neighbors came in to commiserate with the old peasant, who said however: "This may perhaps be a piece of good luck." Months later, the barbarians invaded China and all the young men were drafted into the army, where they met death or captivity by the barbarians—but not the old peasant's crippled son. When the neighbors congratulated the old man on this good fortune he remarked: "Yes, but this may really be a bit of bad luck." Et cetera.

Fables such as this, while charming, are of course especially dear to the hearts of those who have an interest in the continuing passivity of Old Hundred Names. For twenty-five centuries the rulers of China have repeated the Confucian message to their toiling peasantry: "Remain where you are and obey the dictates of heaven!" And the Western merchants took up the refrain from the moment they arrived.

It must be admitted that to nineteenth-century Western eyes the customs of Old Hundred Names seemed a complete reversal of the natural order. China appeared a topsy-turvy land in which the black arrows of compasses pointed to the south instead of the north. Old Hundred Names kept his hat on in company instead of taking it off; his books opened at the end and read from right to left vertically, instead of opening at the beginning and reading from left to right horizontally; he began his meals with dessert and finished them with soup; he placed his guests of honor on his left hand rather than his right; he wore white as a sign of mourning instead of black; drank his wine hot rather than cool; brought the needle to the thread instead of the thread to the needle. Furthermore, in China the Devil was very stupid (you could outwit him by merely placing a screen in front of your door), while in the West the Devil was the master of cunning; in China a written contract was considered a discourteous lack of confidence in a man's given word; in China a girl was married in scarlet clothes rather than in white; in China funerals were noisy affairs instead of solemnly silent occasions. The list was an endless one and, combined with the need to assuage an extremely guilty conscience and justify the harshest kind of exploitation, led to the creation of an absurd but pervasive set of myths regarding China and the Chinese.

For the Westerner in China met Old Hundred Names usually not as a peasant but as a poverty-stricken city worker, willing to work for a few cents a day, humble and submissive, living in conditions of appalling filth and degradation—conditions imposed in part by the Westerner himself. Living in splendid isolation in the foreign settlements of Shanghai or Tientsin or Canton, disporting himself in parks forbidden to Chinese, the Westerner's contact with the teeming millions beyond the settlement gates was limited to his "comprador" (the word is Spanish and means "buyer"), who got him what he wanted from factories to prostitutes, or to the rickshaw boys and coolies waiting outside his exclusive clubs. The Westerner soon gave birth to the comic strip or Fu Manchu school of knowledge about China which is not entirely absent from his think-

". . . the Westerner's contact with the teeming millions . . . was limited to his . . . rickshaw boys and coolies waiting outside his exclusive clubs."

ing even today. An entire dictionary of ridiculous generalizations about China and the Chinese could be composed from this thinking: *Bamboo:* a tree used by torturers (see the movie *China Seas*). *Brigands:* all Chinese peasants are brigands sometimes. *Coolies:* all the Chinese are coolies if they are not brigands. *Detectives:* many Chinese are detectives (see *Charlie Chan*). *Fatalism:* the Chinese are fatalistic (see *The Good Earth*). *Kidnapping:* the Chinese national sport. *Dragon Lady:* Chinese women are strangely wise and extremely beautiful. *Laundrymen:* all Chinese who are not brigands, coolies, or detectives are laundrymen (see *Chinatown*). *Yellow:* the Chinese, being of tawny complexion, are a peril to the white race (see *Yellow Peril*). *Human life:* a commodity of little value in China (see *Fatalism*)—etc.

Even when the Westerner chanced across a generalization which was largely true, he often misinterpreted it. For example, it is true that Old Hundred Names, living in extremely crowded conditions, developed a deep and abiding standard of courtesy—out of necessity as well as inclination. But Chinese courtesy, which is, as anywhere else, thoughtfulness for the rights and feelings of others, was interpreted as a cunning stratagem to "save face." Thus it was understood that Old Hundred Names's pride was so o'erweening that he could not bear to suffer the slightest public disgrace and would often kill himself rather than "lose face." An example of this view is the "Fable of the Poor Man and the Burglar":

One night a thief entered the house of a very poor man. The poor man, who had been asleep, woke up when the thief entered and, in fear, pretended to remain asleep. But the thief had noticed. "He has seen me and knows that I intend to rob him," thought the thief, "but he does not want to wake up and make me lose face. What delicacy of feeling!" So the thief, in gratitude, tiptoed from the house. "What's this?" thought the poor man. "Does this thief think me so poor that he wishes to spare my house? He'll make me lose face before the neighbors!" Bounding out of bed the poor man cried out: "Thief, thief, I am a poor man, but steal something anyhow—even if it is only a pot, or what will my neighbors think of me tomorrow?" It will be noted that this is a story the Chinese tell on themselves.

As for o'erweening pride, there is another fable, about the rich merchant Hou. It seems that Hou always used to refer to himself as extremely stupid and to refer to everything he offered his guests as "very ordinary." One night he gave a huge and expensive feast in the gardens of his palatial house. One of his guests exclaimed: "This is indeed a beautiful moonlight night." Hou bowed and replied: "It is really too kind of you to praise in this way my very great stupidity and I am saddened at being able to offer you tonight only this very ordinary moon." Once again this is Chinese self-satire.

But the idiocy of the Western myths regarding Old Hundred Names is neither charming nor humorous when compared to the facts of Chinese existence under the Western heel. The factories of Shanghai and Canton and Amoy, run by Westerners and their Chinese compradors, were often staffed by eight-year-old children. Children's fingers were more nimble at the cotton looms and their wages were less than ten cents a day—quite a saving for the Western Tai-pan (Big Boss). The children were often sold outright to the factories by their starving parents, and there they worked and lived (if any escaped, then the Chinese overseer in the factory would be fined) until, after a few years, their health had been wrecked and they could be tossed out into the street.

For as taxes multiplied, rents skyrocketed, floods and famines followed each other like phases of the moon, Old Hundred Names increasingly was moving off the land and into the cities all during the nineteenth century. And as urban populations swelled, the world's most atrocious slums spread around Shanghai, Amoy, Canton, Nanking—any Chinese city in which Old Hundred Names could somehow scrabble for a livelihood. Living in pestilential hovels amid garbage-strewn streets, working for pennies a day as a coolie, rickshaw boy, factory hand, or shopkeeper's assistant, he was also allowed the privilege of paying municipal taxes toward the upkeep of the parks and playing fields where Europeans relaxed and from which he was barred.

But the Western presence in China was not always an unmitigated calamity for Old Hundred Names. There were other Westerners besides the Treaty Port merchants and their colonial armies. By the end of the nineteenth century there were more than 750 European Catholic priests and 1,200 Protestant missionaries working in the Celestial Empire. And while their efforts to convert China to Christianity were doomed to failure (by 1900 there were only 500,000 Catholic and less than 60,000 Protestant converts), they did great work in opening hundreds of hospitals (often the first ever seen in the provinces) where Old Hundred Names could find modern medical care for the first time in history, in organizing hundreds of schools where he could learn to read and write his own and other languages, and in attempting to restrain the rapacious appetites of their own countrymen. The influence of missionary ideals and activities, their interest in Old Hundred Names himself as an individual, their initiation of education for women, and their attempt to bring some touch of modernization to the age-old problems of famine and pestilence opened new vistas toward the future. The fact that the missionaries were, in the final analysis, an instrument of Western imperialism is undeniable. So is the fact that there were some four hundred anti-Christian riots in China before the Boxer Rebellion. But the fact that these riots were largely instigated not by workers or peasants but by the jealous landlord-scholar-administrator class would seem to indicate that missionary Christianity was, after all, a very real threat to those who had oppressed Old Hundred Names over the centuries.

NEXT PAGES: *"The factories of Shanghai and Canton and Amoy, run by Westerners and their Chinese compradors, were often staffed by eight-year-old children."*

Nor would it be fair to blame the misery of the Chinese masses entirely on the presence of imperialists. For although Western exploitation of China was thorough and widespread, it was as nothing compared to the exploitation of China by her own ruling classes. The Taiping Rebellion had been directed against the Manchus and the landlord classes, not against the Westerners. It was only when it became apparent to Chinese revolutionaries that Westerners would support the hated Manchu regime that anti-foreign feeling spread among the masses.

For to tell the truth, as the Boxer Rebellion indicated, Old Hundred Names could bear no more. Stimulated by thousands of years of oppression, by the slow influx of Western ideas of liberty and equality, by an intense domestic hatred of his own ruling classes, he was determined to stand on his own feet at last and throw off the yoke. He still hoped that the West might help him—if not, then he would break his own new path into the future. After so many centuries of slumber, China was awakening to a heroic struggle whose convulsions would shake the world.

4

The Son of Heaven Falls to Earth

THE MAN who, more than any other, was to bring about an end to the tyranny under which Old Hundred Names groaned was born in 1866 in a village named Choy Hang (the Blue Expanse of the Kingfisher), south of Canton. It is said that just before his birth his mother had a dream in which the God Pei Ti appeared to her. The God seemed to be enraged because the child she was about to bear would one day do him harm. To ward off this omen of evil, when the child was born his mother named him Tai-cheong (Servant of God). In China it is customary to give infants a name which they will use only during childhood. But just to make doubly sure, Tai-cheong's mother gave him the name Yat-sen for his adult years. Yat-sen means Spirit of Tranquility. The family name was Sun. Unfortunately for his mother's superstition, but fortunately for the people of China, Sun Yat-sen was one day to topple the God Pei Ti and to pass his life in anything but a spirit of tranquility.

Sun Yat-sen

The Sun family was very poor when Yat-sen was born. His father had been a tailor who found few customers. But some local missionaries persuaded the elder Sun to become a Bible salesman. Yat-sen's father was, accordingly, baptized a Christian. By 1866 the Sun family owned a small piece of land in Choy Hang and were reckoned middle-class peasants by their neighbors. Later, with more passion than accuracy, Sun Yat-sen was to declare: "I am a coolie and the son of a coolie. I was born with the poor and I am still poor. My sympathies have always been with the struggling masses."

Two coincidental but decisive influences on Sun Yat-sen's life derived from the region in which he was born. The provinces around Canton had been, for many years, the scene of widespread emigration to foreign lands. Foreign companies, in search of cheap labor, hired south China peasants under exploitive contracts and shipped them abroad. During the 1850's, for example, many thousands had been taken to the United States, where they formed the chief source of labor for the construction of the Union Pacific Railroad. Many more thousands went to work in Malaya and Indonesia. Over the years a surprisingly large proportion of these overseas Chinese attained some degree of success and prosperity. They sent money home and often paid to have the younger members of their families educated abroad. It was also in south China and especially in the provinces around Canton that the Taiping Rebellion had first mushroomed. In fact, many Cantonese emigrants were themselves Taiping survivors who were fleeing Manchu vengeance. And among those who remained at home the Taiping Rebellion was still a living memory. As Sun Yat-sen grew up in his native village, he listened endlessly to the talk of the elders who reminisced about that mighty uprising, about how they had come so very close to establishing a China of the common man, and of how and why they had failed.

Sun's elder brother had emigrated to Hawaii some years before, and when Sun showed ability and promise at the local village school, this brother paid for his passage to Hawaii and placed him in an Anglican school in Honolulu. Sun was fourteen at the time and this was his first direct contact with the West. He studied English, mathematics, and English history. He learned about England's constitutional democracy, sang in the school choir, and conceived a desire to become a Christian. When he was graduated in 1882, young Sun won second prize in English grammar and was considered a lad of marked ability by the school authorities. That same year Sun Yat-sen returned home where both his ways and ideas were considered scandalously radical. In frustrated anger at the symbols of ignorance and oppression, he nearly broke a finger trying to knock the head off the idol of the God Pei Ti (just as the God had predicted he would do). His father paid for the damage and, with more financial help from the elder brother in Hawaii, packed young Sun (he was eighteen) off to the American-operated Canton Medical College, where he would study to become a doctor. Later, Sun transferred to the British-operated Queen Victoria Medical College in Hong Kong. Here, in 1884, he became a Christian and at the same time dutifully married a girl from his own village whom he had never seen and who remained at home as a proper daughter-in-law.

One of the periodic French imperialistic rampages in China (in 1885) seems to have first roused Sun's interest in national reform and salvation. He joined the secret Triad Society, which had inherited the White Lotus tradition of rebellion against the Manchus, and resolved to press on with his medical studies—but for reasons having little to do with medicine. "I became determined to overthrow the Manchu Dynasty and establish a Republic," Sun later wrote. "I became a doctor in order to have free access everywhere." From 1887 to 1892 Sun was a student of a young British missionary doctor, James Cantlie, at Hong Kong. He studied chemistry, botany, physics, physiology, clinical surgery, and medicine and learned to play cricket with Cantlie. When he was graduated he attempted to set up a medical practice in Macao, a port city near Canton.

Macao had been for centuries a Portuguese colony, and in order to preserve their monopoly on medical practice, the Portuguese authorities forbade Sun to practice without a diploma from Portugal. Abandoning his new profession, Sun traveled to north China in 1893. He had already organized a modest secret society of his own, the Revive China Society, and with the help of his friends he sent petitions to the Manchu government urging them to establish schools and universities. The petitions were, of course, ignored.

In 1894 Sun Yat-sen embarked on his life's work—which was nothing less than the destruction of the Imperial government and the creation of a new life for the Chinese people. He expanded his secret society, establishing Revive China branches (each cell had fifteen members who were sworn to each other by blood oath) in various cities throughout the Celestial Empire. When the Japanese onslaught of 1895 shocked China into an awareness of her weakness, Sun Yat-sen was already a recognized revolutionary leader. He received financial help from a Shanghai merchant named Charles Jones Soong who had lived many years in the United States and was a Methodist and a graduate in theology of Vanderbilt University. This remarkable man and his even more remarkable family were to have a tremendously important influence on the life of Sun Yat-sen and on the course of Chinese history down to the present day.

Sun's first attempt at direct action was made in 1895. Using Hong Kong as a base of operations, the conspirators attempted to seize the Canton provincial government offices. The plot was discovered, Sun's friends were tortured and killed, and Sun himself was forced to flee in disguise (he cut off his pigtail and grew a mustache) to Japan. While in Japan he used the name Nakayama (*Chung Shan* in Chinese), meaning Central Mountain. He also made contact with various Japanese groups who, for their own reasons, were interested in seeing the Manchu Dynasty collapse. The Japanese Black Dragon Society, hoping that Sun's activities would weaken the Celestial Empire, gave him substantial financial aid during the next ten years.

In 1896 Sun went to Honolulu, where he lectured to the Chinese colony and founded the Society of Enthusiasm for China, and then proceeded to the United States. There he established close contacts with the Chinese of San Francisco, New York, and other cities and, incidentally, studied American democracy in action during one of its more corrupt periods. That same year he went on to England—and was promptly kidnapped by the Chinese Embassy in London. For the Manchu Dynasty was growing alarmed at the activities of this young traveler. There was a price on his head. What awaited him if the embassy succeeded in shipping him back to China, Sun knew only too well. "I faced the prospect," he later wrote, "of having, to start with, my ankles crushed in a press and broken with hammer blows, my eyelids cut off and, eventually, of being hacked into small pieces." Sun prayed while a prisoner at the embassy. He also bribed a valet and managed to get word of his plight to his old instructor, Doctor (now Sir) James Cantlie. The good doctor descended on the London press, the Foreign Office, and the House of Commons to such effect that within a few days Sun Yat-sen was freed. Undaunted by his experience Sun traveled on to France.

What Sun Yat-sen learned from his tour of the Western democracies was that democratic process does not always ensure the well-being of a nation's citizens. "A sole preoccupation with the wealth and strength of the nation," he wrote, "and not with the powers of the people makes it impossible for humanity to achieve its maximum happiness." He returned to Asia.

Singapore, Tokyo, Hanoi, Hong Kong—everywhere Sun traveled he preached the doctrine of a new China, founded newspapers, collected funds, made recruits, and strengthened his following. He returned to China from time to time, sometimes disguised as a coolie, sometimes as a peddler or a stevedore. In 1900, having founded yet another secret society (the Society for the Abolition of the Mandate), he once more attempted direct action. Rounding up support among dissident army officers, he tried to seize Canton. One of the conspirators planted a mine beneath the house of the Imperial viceroy in Canton. But the mine failed to explode and nearly asphyxiated the officer, who was captured, tortured, and executed. "Each time I think of him," Sun later wrote, "I stand up respectfully." The conspiracy was a failure.

But 1900 was also the year of the Boxer Rebellion (with which Sun had no connection), of Western vengeance, and of the final weakening of the Manchu Dynasty. It marked the beginning of the end of Imperial rule in China. When the old Dowager Empress returned to Peking (a burned, looted, and thoroughly cowed capital) from her flight to the interior in 1902 and persuaded the skeptical Western powers that her regime still remained their best hope of exploiting a peaceful China, foreign troops remained in Peking as "legation guards" and foreign troops remained stationed all along the railroad line from Peking to the sea. Not only the United States Marine Legation Guard, but also the 15th Regiment of the United States Infantry was a part of these international forces. Thus to many Chinese it seemed that only foreign arms continued the Manchus in power.

The belated and tentative reforms carried out by the dynasty— such as the educational reform which abolished the old government examinations, the organization of a cabinet (responsible only to the Empress), and the placing of relatively liberal men in some government posts—only served to weaken the authority of the dynasty, while it could do nothing to mask Manchu subservience to foreign power.

During the following years, Sun Yat-sen continued his revolutionary attempts. The Peking government had placed a price of $750,000 on his head. And if Sun's plots failed one after the other (he failed more than a dozen times), he somehow managed to escape capture. In 1905 Sun Yat-sen summed up his ideas in the Three Principles of the People. These principles may be roughly translated as: the life of the people through work; the power of the people through democracy; the independence of the people through nationalism. "The people must be convinced," Sun wrote, "that there has never been any other power than that which it bestows." It was also in 1905 that Sun amalgamated various revolutionary secret societies into the Tung Meng Hui (Together-Sworn Society) of which he became president. The new organization used some ancient techniques (members were known to each other only by number, communicated only verbally, made themselves known by such devices as lifting a teacup with their thumb and two fingers or pausing on the threshold of a room and advancing left foot first, etc.) and some modern ones—they published a newspaper from their base in Japan called *Min Pao* (the People) which was smuggled by the thousands to mainland China.

But the Manchu dragon still had a sharp tooth or two. When, in 1906, one of Sun's revolutionary attempts failed, Peking diplomats were able to persuade the Japanese government to expel the revolutionists it had been harboring. Once again Sun Yat-sen found himself roaming the world in search of support. In addition, the Manchus had undertaken to reform their army. Under the leadership of a new commander, Yuan Shih-kai, modern training methods and new arms were introduced. A large group of new officers were appointed—mainly drawn from Chinese who had studied abroad —many of whom had been heavily influenced by Sun Yat-sen's revolutionary thought. The Manchu New Army was therefore very definitely a two-edged blade which might cut the wielder as well as the victim.

In 1908 the Empress finally died. The new Emperor, Pu Yi, was an infant, and Manchu authority was exercised by a prince regent. But the weakening of Manchu power was illustrated by the fact that when, in 1910, a revolutionary bomb plot to kill the Prince Regent was uncovered, its leader, Wang Ching-wei, a follower of Sun Yat-sen, was not executed, merely imprisoned. Sun Yat-sen himself was abroad at the time on one of his world tours in endless quest for money and recruits. In October of 1911, Sun found himself in Denver, Colorado, where he was to lecture on the hope of building a new China. He received a cable from Hankow which was, of course, in code. But Sun had shipped his code book ahead and could not decipher the message.

The coded message was nothing less than an announcement that the revolution had finally begun. And, typically, it had begun by accident. A group of Sun's followers had been preparing for one of their endless bomb plots in the city of Wuchang, across the Yangtze River from Hankow. The conspirators had established themselves in the tsarist Russian compound of Wuchang where they would be free from Manchu police. There they busily manufactured bombs. Suddenly, on October 9, 1911, one of their bombs accidentally exploded. Immediately the authorities searched their hideout and found long lists of names of members of the conspiracy. Obviously something would have to be done and done quickly if they were to escape Imperial vengeance. That night, the revolutionaries made contact with units of the Manchu New Army stationed in Hankow, and on the following morning, October 10, 1911, a unit of engineers rose in revolt. They faced down very light resistance on the part of some of the other troops in Hankow, but for the most part the New Army regiments in the city went over to the revolutionary cause. The Imperial viceroy in Hankow fled; his palace was in flames and numbers of his Manchu associates were killed. The date October 10 has ever since been celebrated in China as the birthday of the republic, the "double ten" (tenth day of the tenth month).

Meanwhile, in Colorado, Sun had finally caught up with his code book. Since the cable which told of the Hankow uprising also said that the revolutionists were low on funds, Sun composed a cable in which he advised putting off the attempt. But the next morning he read in the newspapers that the Chinese revolution was in full swing and that much of southern China had gone over to the republican cause. Sun's cable was never sent. Instead he immediately rushed to London, where he was able to persuade the British government not to interfere and, more importantly, to prevent the Japanese government from interfering. Events in China moved with amazing rapidity. The rebels had seized the city of Nanking and there they established a provisional government. When Sun was notified that he had been elected provisional President of this government, he immediately rebaptized his country. China, which for thousands of years had called itself the Middle Empire, now became the People's Flowery Middle State. Returning to China, Sun was duly elected President of the new republic by the Nanking National Assembly.

But unfortunately for Sun's cause, the People's Flowery Middle State exercised no power in the north—around Peking and Manchuria. There, seeing which way the wind blew, Yuan Shih-kai,

Yuan Shih-kai

commander of the Manchu New Army, seized power for himself. The Prince Regent had resigned in December and Yuan's army was the only power in north China. Unlike Sun, Yuan had at his back a well-trained and relatively powerful army. While Sun's followers still lacked funds, Yuan had plenty of money. Perhaps of most importance, Yuan Shih-kai, a military adventurer, a typical "strong man" who thought little about politics but much about power, was a figure more familiar to Western diplomats than the "doctrinaire revolutionary" Sun Yat-sen. Yuan would, the Western powers assumed, bring order out of what appeared to be chaos. And with their large investments in China, order was what the Westerners wanted. Furthermore, Yuan was more acceptable to the Japanese militarists who posed the most immediate threat to Chinese sovereignty.

Fully aware of all these contingencies, Sun Yat-sen, hoping to influence Yuan to act democratically, entered into negotiations with him. If the military commander would agree to support the new republic, Sun was willing to step down from the Presidency. Yuan agreed and on February 12, 1912, the Manchu Dynasty and its infant Emperor, Pu Yi, formally abdicated the celestial throne. Yuan Shih-kai was proclaimed President of the Chinese Republic at the capital in Peking.

Yuan Shih-kai, despite his New Army, lacked sufficient military power to control the independent bodies of troops raised by local landlords throughout China for their own protection. Nor did he have enough money to bribe them into loyalty. Therefore, he had little choice but to legalize these private armies by making their commanders governors in their respective provinces. In this way the seeds were sown for the twentieth-century warlord era in Chinese history. This phenomenon—of locally powerful private armies at the disposition of their own generals, sometimes cooperating with the central government, more often not, disposed to banditry and to the cruelest kind of oppression toward local peasants—was one which would continue until the conquest of power by the Communists. It was based, essentially, upon the ease with which peasants could be conscripted into local forces and the ease with which those forces could be supplied with food in their own territories. In addition, many of China's provinces were, due to geographical reasons, far easier to defend than to attack. Mountain ranges and broad river barriers provided effective obstacles to central government power. And very often local warlords received support, either secret or open, from Western nations or Japan. For the next thirty years no Chinese government would be able to maintain itself without the support of a warlord coalition in one combination or another.

The 1911 revolution had, in fact, overthrown nothing but the Manchu Dynasty. In the central capital ruled a military dictator, Yuan Shih-kai; in the provincial capitals ruled local warlords; in the villages the landlords remained all-powerful. Led by intellectuals and by the Chinese community abroad, the 1911 revolution left the vast masses of China relatively untouched. For them nothing had changed but their top masters. The only immediate sign of change in China was the sudden disappearance of millions of pig-tails as the population finally relieved itself of this symbol of sub-jugation to the Manchus.

In 1912, at Nanking, one of Sun Yat-sen's followers, Sung Chiao-jen, established from the many secret societies and organizations under Sun's control the Kuomintang (National People's Party) as an open political party along Western lines. Although Sun Yat-sen disapproved of this step as imprudent, he did not oppose Sung Chiao-jen's actions. Kuomintang delegates appeared at Peking to cooperate with Yuan Shih-kai's ministers and to work toward con-trolling the new government through the usual democratic processes. But Yuan Shih-kai responded by having his agents assassinate Sung Chiao-jen. Sun himself escaped once more to Japan (in 1913) and, when he heard that the Kuomintang delegates in Peking had been imprisoned and the party suppressed, wrote to Yuan accusing him of high treason. Yuan responded by nominating himself emperor early in 1915. But powerful though he was, the strong man was not powerful enough to reimpose the hated Imperial system. He soon retracted his Imperial claims.

Sun Yat-sen now returned to China and established headquarters at Canton. Also in 1915, he married for the second time—choosing for his wife one of the three daughters of Charles Jones Soong, the merchant who had aided him for so many years. Soong Ching-ling was to remain devoted to her husband until his death and to his ideals thereafter.

Meanwhile, distant Europe had plunged into the nightmare of World War I. It was, of course, none of China's business. Never-theless, the Western powers put on pressure and China found her-self at war with Germany and Austria-Hungary. More than 140,000 Chinese coolies were hired to go to Europe—to dig trenches and perform other heavy labor—since in the European view that was all

Madame Sun Yat-sen

they were good for. And in Asia, Japan, who was also allied with England and France against the Central Powers, seized the German concessions in China's Shantung peninsula. There, with British backing, she was to remain. To take further advantage of Europe's preoccupation with its own bloodletting, Japan presented the Peking government with a list of twenty-one "demands." These demands, ranging over a broad field of treaty port rights, economic privileges, and usurpations of Chinese authority, were an intolerable imposition upon a still sovereign nation. Although old Yuan Shih-kai tried to resist the demands, eventually there was nothing to do but swallow the bitter pill.

Yuan Shih-kai's death in 1916 left central power in China divided among various warlords in the provinces and the badly battered Kuomintang in its Canton enclave. After Yuan's death there was even an attempt, with Japanese backing, to restore the Manchu Dynasty in the person of the child Emperor Pu Yi. But the celestial rule, in the face of an explosion of rioting and popular indignation, lasted only a few days before the Emperor and his followers had to seek sanctuary in the Japanese legation in Peking. Thereafter, the warlord coalitions came and went at Peking with monotonous regularity and tiresome confusion. The hope of a modern, national China remained now only with Sun Yat-sen and his followers in Canton.

The collapse of central authority in China was not entirely a bad thing. With government police uncertain as to who was giving orders and with a general breakdown in what little efficiency had previously been displayed, Chinese students and intellectuals found themselves relatively safe to read, write, and speak what they thought. The National University at Peking became the center of a Chinese intellectual renaissance. Some of the naïveté of the hopes of Chinese students shines through the exhortations of Chen Tu-hsiu, an intellectual newly returned from France, who published a magazine called *La Jeunesse* (Youth). "In order to support Mr. Democracy," wrote Chen, "we are obliged to oppose Confucianism, the code of rituals, chastity, traditional ethics, old politics; and in order to support Mr. Science, we are compelled to oppose traditional arts, traditional religion; and in order to support Mr. Democracy and Mr. Science, we simply have to oppose the so-called national heritage and old literature."

This outburst of optimism was explained to a large extent by the entrance of the United States into the First World War. President Woodrow Wilson enunciated his famous "Fourteen Points" on which peace was to be based and his words found instant response in China. Did not the American President speak of "open covenants of peace openly arrived at"; of the self-determination of peoples?

Did he not speak with the voice of true democracy? No doubt, after the war ended, the Western democracies would dismantle their imperialist controls over China and, led by American idealism, allow China to develop peacefully toward unity and plenty.

The awakening was rude. When the victorious Allies met at Versailles to dictate the new world order, a Chinese request that Japan's twenty-one demands be cancelled was ignored. The Chinese representatives fought against the continued Japanese occupation of the Shantung peninsula (Japan finally relinquished her grip on this former German territory in 1921), but the dealing and bargaining at Versailles made plain the fact that whatever noble words they may have uttered during the war, the European powers had no intention of relaxing their viselike grip on China or other colonial areas.

"When the news of the Paris Peace Conference finally reached us," wrote a Chinese student, "we were greatly shocked. We at once awoke to the fact that foreign nations were still selfish and militaristic and that they were all great liars. . . . We came to the conclusion that a greater World War would come sooner or later, and that this great war would be fought in the East. . . . Looking at our people and at the pitiful ignorant masses, we couldn't help but feel that we should struggle."

On May 4, 1919, more than five thousand Chinese students and intellectuals marched through the streets of Peking shouting: "Cancel the twenty-one demands!" "Down with Japan!" and "Down with power politics!" They invaded the foreign legation compounds to angrily demand that American and British diplomats live up to Wilson's words and help them against Japanese encroachment. The police soon dispersed the demonstrators, arresting many. But what came to be known as the "May 4th Movement" gave a powerful stimulus to Sun Yat-sen's untiring efforts to widen the base of his Kuomintang Party. It also marked a turning point in Chinese revolutionary struggle. For if the Western powers had betrayed China at Versailles, there was one Western power which had not even been invited to attend that peace conference—the newly established Union of Soviet Socialist Republics.

In 1910, Vladimir Lenin, in exile in Switzerland and busy with the building of the Russian Bolshevik Party, had said: "Each point in Sun Yat-sen's program is conceived in a democratic spirit which is both combative and sincere." Now, in 1921, with the Bolsheviks triumphant in Russia and with China in chaos, Sun Yat-sen finally turned from the Western powers who for so long had opposed his attempt to introduce democracy and social justice into the warlord-ridden Chinese republic to open negotiations with the young Soviet Union. In August, 1921, Sun sent a letter to G. V. Chicherin, People's Commissar of Foreign Affairs in Moscow. ". . . I would like to enter into personal contact with you and my friends in Moscow," he wrote. "I am extremely interested in your work and particularly in the organization of your soviets, your army, and educational system."

How desperately Sun needed help was amply illustrated by an incident which took place in Canton. That great port city, Kuomintang headquarters, had been occupied by the forces of a local warlord named Chen Chiung-ming, who invited Sun Yat-sen to remain in Canton and establish the city as the Nationalist capital of China. In return for Chen Chiung-ming's support, Sun had to name him governor of the province. But what choice did Sun have? With no armed forces at his disposal and continually at the mercy of the shifting warlord regimes at Peking who claimed to be China's legal government, Sun had to make whatever deal he could with Chen. However, what the policy of relying upon warlord support could mean was demonstrated on June 16, 1922, when Chen Chiung-ming suddenly turned against Sun and his government. The warlord's troops imprisoned all the Kuomintang officials they could find, killed those who resisted, surrounded Sun Yat-sen's house, and would have killed him too had he not taken refuge on a gunboat, where, with many of his associates, he had to spend fifty-six days as a refugee from his former supporter.

But with the introduction of the Soviet Union into Chinese affairs, events were quickly to take a new and dramatically decisive turn. Sun Yat-sen's revolution had proceeded piecemeal. Lacking real military power and a strong financial base, it was running into the sands of Chinese factionalism and counterrevolution. Now a new road into the future suddenly appeared before the harassed Chinese revolutionaries. It was a dangerous road, beset by pitfalls—but it was one which would eventually lead them to their goal.

5

United Front, Divided Aims

At the end of July, 1921, nine men held a secret meeting on the top floor of a private school for girls in the French concession of Shanghai. They were alone in the building (the girls being on summer holiday) except for a cook on the ground floor who also acted as a sentinel to warn against any uninvited guests. The nine men were young Chinese intellectuals who represented various Marxist study groups in China. They had gathered together for this secret meeting in order to found a Chinese Communist Party. As chairman of the meeting the group elected Chang Kuo-tao, a student recently returned from Japan, and as secretaries Chou Fu-hai, another student, and Mao Tse-tung, son of a Hunanese peasant, who had become interested in Marxism while studying at Peking University. The group soon fell into an argument as to what their new party's policy ought to be. Some of those present maintained that the Chinese working class was too immature and scanty to form

Mao Tse-tung

the basis of a real Communist movement and therefore the party policy must be one of striving for the establishment of a middle-class democracy first. Others argued that the party aim should be to summon a revolution and establish a dictatorship of the working class at once. But a majority of the delegates rejected both these extremes. They decided that the Chinese Communist Party must fight for the eventual establishment of a working-class dictatorship, but that for the next few years it would have to collaborate with the Kuomintang Party in the struggle for freedom from foreign domination and for the establishment of a unified government. Their deliberations went on for four days—but at the end of that time they were interrupted by the sudden appearance of "a suspicious person in a long coat." The delegates quickly grabbed their documents and fled. Ten minutes later the police arrived to find the meeting place deserted.

The delegates (their number increased to twelve) reconvened a few days later on a boat in the middle of a lake at Hangchow (near Shanghai). There they continued their debate as to what their attitude toward Sun Yat-sen and the Kuomintang Party ought to be. The more militant among them argued that Sun and his Kuomintang represented the middle class and were therefore in direct opposition to the aims of Communism. For this reason the Chinese Communist Party ought to display the same hostility toward Sun Yat-sen's movement as it did toward the warlord government of Peking. But once again the moderates present won out. They decided that while criticizing the "false teachings" of Sun Yat-sen and trying to maneuver Communists into positions of influence, they would collaborate with him and with the Kuomintang in its practical struggle against the warlords and foreign imperialism.

In reaching this conclusion, the young student Communists who met at Shanghai accurately reflected the considered decisions of the Second Congress of the Communist International which had met in Moscow during the summer of 1920. At that congress, delegates from Communist parties throughout the world had heard Lenin and his associates call upon them to throw their energies into the fight for liberation of colonial areas from imperialist domination. And if this policy suited the feelings of the assembled delegates from India, East Asia, Africa, and the Middle East, it also filled an urgent need of the newly established Bolshevik government of Russia.

Vladimir Lenin was, above all, an extremely practical man. Karl Marx and Friedrich Engels, the founders of the modern Communist movement, had always held that a Communist revolution, since it must be based on a working class, would come first in the most industrially advanced nations—where the working class was best educated, best organized, and where the extremity of difference between working-class conditions and capitalist profits would be greatest. Lenin had found ways of adapting Marx's teachings to furnish theoretical support for a Communist revolution in Russia, industrially one of the most backward of nations, with a relatively small working class and a very large peasant population. But basically, Communist theory remained rooted in the conception that a peasant society (such as the Chinese) must first of all establish capitalism (the private ownership of the means of production) before capitalism could be overthrown. Communism (the communal ownership of the means of production) could hardly be established in a country where there were no means of production. Therefore, on the best theoretical basis, Communist parties in such colonial and unindustrialized societies as the Chinese would have to work with the middle-class democratic parties toward the establishment of that very type of society which they eventually hoped to overthrow. But as we have noted, Lenin was a practical man. His reasons for urging the cooperation of Communist movements with middle-class parties in such relatively backward countries as China were immediate and concrete as well as theoretical.

Russia, which was only now emerging from the throes of civil war, and which had suffered large-scale intervention by British, French, American, and Japanese troops in her internal affairs, still felt threatened by what she viewed as the encirclement and aggressive plots of capitalist countries against her fledgling Communist experiment. To offset this threat, Lenin and his followers had expected a wave of Communist revolutions throughout Europe to follow the Russian success. The wave had come—and gone, leaving extremely reactionary forces in control of such Russian neighbors as Poland, Germany, and the Balkan states. The energies of the capitalist countries would have to be directed elsewhere, if possible. Furthermore, it was an article of Communist faith that imperial powers such as Britain and France depended to a large extent upon the exploitation of semicolonial countries like China for much of their wealth. If the Asiatic markets could be closed to such countries they would be profoundly weakened—and pose less of a threat to the Soviet Union itself. Since a Communist revolution in the land-and-peasant-oriented Asiatic societies was not to be expected in the near future, Communist aims would have to be achieved through support of the anti-imperialistic, nationalist-democratic movements in these countries which gave promise of throwing off the yoke of foreign exploitation. This by no means meant that Communist parties in China and India, for example, should not propagate their doctrines among the people or fail to organize effective political machines. It simply meant that for the immediate future they would have to pursue their long-term aims through support of such movements as Sun Yat-sen's Kuomintang.

To give practical effect to Lenin's viewpoint, the Soviet Union did three things: it helped Chinese students and intellectuals to found the Chinese Communist Party; it established communications with Sun Yat-sen directly; it opened formal negotiations with the warlord government in Peking regarding the status of former tsarist Russian rights and privileges in China.

On the twenty-fifth of July, 1919, the new Soviet Union had issued a declaration to the government and people of China in which it offered to do away with all the previous special concessions and privileges which the tsar's government had forced on China. During the negotiations which followed, various difficulties arose. The Peking government was unable to wrest from Russian control all of what had been lost to the tsar. But by 1924 agreement was reached, and the treaty which resulted was far more favorable to China than the treaties which had long since been imposed by Britain, France, and Japan.

The diplomat chosen by Moscow to negotiate with the warlord government in Peking, Adolf A. Joffe, also established contact with Sun Yat-sen. After conversations between them in Shanghai during the month of January, 1923, a joint communiqué was issued: "Dr. Sun Yat-sen considers that the Communist order or even the Soviet system cannot be effectually introduced into China and that it would have no success. This view is entirely shared by Mr. Joffe, who is, rather, of the opinion that the first and most pressing Chinese problem is the realization of national unity and complete independence. In this great task he has assured Dr. Sun Yat-sen that China has the sincere sympathy of the Soviet people and can count on the help of the Soviet Union." Commenting, Sun Yat-sen said: "We no longer bother about the countries of the West. Our faces are turned toward Soviet Russia."

On February 21, 1923, Sun Yat-sen, with the help of three rival warlords, regained control of the city of Canton from Chen Chiung-ming, the treacherous warlord from whom he had fled. It was from Canton that he sent, during the following summer, a young Chinese army officer named Chiang Kai-shek to Russia to study the organization and methods of the Soviet Red Army—and it was at Canton on October 6, 1923, that he received his principal Soviet adviser, Mikhail Borodin.

Although Borodin had been born and raised in Russia, like many of his generation of Bolshevik revolutionists he had traveled extensively. Mexico, Europe, and America had been on his itinerary. He had lived for more than ten years in the United States, spent six months in prison in Glasgow, and was considered one of the Russian Communist Party's ablest agents. After conversations between Sun and Borodin which extended over a period of weeks, Borodin was appointed as a special adviser to the Kuomintang. Slowly he built up a small staff of Soviet advisers and technical experts and hammered out a new program and a new structure for the Kuomintang.

Basically, the most valuable advice Borodin could give Sun Yat-sen was that if he wanted to defeat the old order in China—the landlord-warlord coalition supported by foreign imperialists—he would somehow have to mobilize the great weight of the Chinese

Mikhail Borodin

masses and throw them into the struggle. Accordingly, with Sun's agreement, in January of 1924, the First Congress of the Kuomintang Party, held at Canton, adopted a new constitution (written by Borodin himself) and a new policy. Henceforth the party was to exercise strict discipline, undertake direct propaganda among the peasants and industrial workers through trained agitators, and build its own army, thereby eliminating reliance on the vagaries of the warlords.

Meanwhile, the Chinese Communist Party had urged its members, of whom there were very, very few—500 in 1922, about 1,200 in 1924—to join the Kuomintang as individuals, while maintaining their membership in their own party. It was hoped that Communists within the Kuomintang would be able to influence decisions and gradually effect a "reform from above," while the Communist Party continued to expand its influence among the peasants and workers to seek "reform from below." In elections held for the setting up of the first Central Executive Committee of the Kuomintang (an organ modeled on Russian advice), the Communists won three of the twenty-four seats.

In May, 1924, Borodin, joined later by General "Galen," a Soviet military adviser whose real name was V. K. Blücher, supervised the establishment of the Whampoa Military Academy for the training of Kuomintang officers. The first commandant of the new academy was Chiang Kai-shek, the young officer whom Sun had sent to Russia the previous summer. Later that same year (in October) the first of many shipments of Russian arms and military supplies reached Canton.

Meantime, the old warlord coalition in Peking was undergoing another of its periodic upheavals. Fighting had broken out on September 16, 1924, between the Peking warlords and the Manchurian warlord Chang Tso-lin. Seeing a chance to win possibly decisive support for his program, Sun Yat-sen announced his support of Chang Tso-lin, who won the capital in a combination of intricate political deals and battles. Although Sun entered Peking on Christmas Day, 1924, Chang Tso-lin remained in control of the city and proved no more amenable than any other warlord to Sun's program. In any event, Sun did not survive long enough to solve this problem. Even as he entered Peking, Sun was suffering from a liver attack. He took to his bed and the doctors diagnosed cancer of the liver. Sun Yat-sen was fifty-eight years old and he was never to get up again. He died on March 12, 1925—one of the few leaders in the long, long history of China to die a poor man. As he lay on his deathbed, Sun Yat-sen gave his assent to a "will" composed by Wang Ching-wei, intended as his final bequest to the Chinese nation and to history.

In his will Sun repeated his Three Principles of the People: national independence, democracy, and the people's livelihood, as

Chang Tso-lin with his grandsons

well as three policies to bring these principles into being: effective anti-imperialism, cooperation with the Soviet Union, and encouragement of the workers' and peasants' movements.

"For forty years," the will stated, "I have devoted myself to the cause of the people's revolution with but one end in view: the elevation of China to a position of freedom and equality among the nations. My experiences during these forty years have convinced me that to attain this goal we must bring about an awakening among our own people and ally ourselves in a common struggle with those peoples of the world who treat us as equals.

Chiang Kai-shek

"The Revolution is not yet finished. Let all our comrades follow my plan for National Reconstruction. . . ."

With the death of Sun Yat-sen, leadership of the Kuomintang devolved more and more onto the shoulders of Chiang Kai-shek, the young officer who ran the Whampoa Military Academy and who had been one of Sun's closest associates. Chiang Chou-tai, who had been given the nickname of Kai-shek (firm as a rock) in his youth, was born on October 31, 1887, in the village of Chi-kou in Chekiang Province. His family was relatively wealthy, having made a small fortune in the salt and tea trade. In 1906 Chiang Kai-shek entered the Imperial Military Academy outside Peking. But after only one year of study there he left to attend the Japanese Imperial Military College at Tokyo. There he spent four years in study, learning Japanese and making many acquaintances both among Japanese leaders and among the exiled Chinese revolutionists led by Sun Yat-sen. By 1910 Chiang Kai-shek had become a follower of Sun's movement and he played a small part in the Kuomintang military attempts to seize power in 1911 and 1913. During World War I, Chiang spent his time running a small brokerage business in Shanghai, but with the death of Yuan Shih-kai (the warlord who had seized power after the Manchu downfall), Chiang once more joined Sun Yat-sen's movement and, as one of the few trained army officers in Sun's entourage, rapidly gained a position of trust and influence within the newly born Kuomintang. His real career did not start, however, until 1923, when Sun sent him to Moscow to study and observe the Soviet Red Army. Chiang's reactions to this visit, which lasted only three months, were somewhat obscure. At first, upon his return and for some years thereafter, he announced himself (publicly, at least) as deeply impressed by Soviet methods and enthusiastic for the Communist reconstruction of Russian society. But many years later, after his split with the Chinese Communist Party, he maintained that he had always been suspicious of Soviet intentions and had been disillusioned with Communist life during his visit. But in 1925 Chiang Kai-shek needed both Soviet supplies (about $2,000,000 worth had reached Canton from Vladivostock by December, 1925) and guidance—which was still supplied by Borodin and General Galen and their staffs.

To both the Russian advisers and the Chinese Communist Party, support of the Kuomintang, now that it was led by Chiang Kai-shek, was a problem of growing dimensions. As a military man whose background was almost entirely that of the upper middle class, Chiang was viewed with suspicion in Moscow. And since his opinions seemed to waver with events, he was suspected by Chinese Communists and by the more militantly revolutionary wing of the

Kuomintang as being too much of an opportunist. But to abandon Chiang meant abandoning the Chinese revolution, while to attempt to replace him would lead to a split, and very possibly a minor civil war within the Kuomintang itself. Although there would be endless argument and squabbling over it, Moscow, the Chinese Communist Party, and the Russian advisers maintained the view that Chiang must be supported, at least until the Peking warlord government had been routed and foreign imperialism defeated. But the internal bickerings of Communists and left-wing Kuomintang members over just how much and how far they would support Chiang really reflected much deeper problems which were only now beginning to emerge.

After Sun Yat-sen's untimely death in Peking, the Kuomintang, led by Chiang Kai-shek, and with Soviet supplies and advice, began that two-year battling march to power which became known as the Great Northern Expedition. With a small army trained in modern tactics, and with shifting alliances among the warlords, Chiang defeated one warlord after another as he advanced from Canton northward to the Yangtze valley. By 1926-1927 practically all of southern China was under Kuomintang rule and Chiang's armies were poised to strike both at Peking and at Shanghai.

A very important element in Chiang's success was the adoption of the Soviet tactic of sending political agitators and organizers ahead of the military forces to convert or demoralize opposing troops. Many of these agitators were Communists; some were Kuomintang agents. But all of them preached the same things to the oppressed peasants and city workers in the path of Chiang's armies—nationalism, unity, and an end to foreign domination. Another important weapon was bribery. Warlords attempting to oppose the Kuomintang advance found the entire countryside rebelling against them; worse than that, they found their own troops going over to the Kuomintang side in droves. In the larger towns and cities, organized workers would seize control just before the arrival of Chiang's forces, making resistance impossible. The Great Northern Expedition was, in fact, nothing less than a Nationalist revolution throughout southern China. Nor did the foreign powers fail to provide fuel for Nationalist propaganda. At Shanghai, Canton, Hong Kong, and other Treaty Ports, European police opened fire on Chinese worker-student demonstrations. These provocations were inevitably followed by Chinese counterdemonstrations (such as the Chinese boycott against British goods which developed in Hong Kong in 1925-1926) and the fires of Chinese anti-imperialistic feeling grew hotter, lending new strength to the Kuomintang.

Of much greater importance in the long run, however, was the fact that among the peasants, the Nationalist revolution was looked upon not simply as a fight for national unity and against imperialism, but as a real revolution which ought to make the land theirs and end the landlord domination of their villages. Ahead of and behind the advancing Nationalist armies, peasant uprisings began to spread like wildfire in the southern provinces. This growing peasant revolutionary movement posed a fundamental problem to the Kuomintang and to the Chinese Communist Party. The Communists were bound to support Chiang Kai-shek and the Kuomintang. But many of the Kuomintang leaders and officers were themselves landlords. Others were big-city merchants and bankers. All of these were absolutely opposed to any revolution which would undermine their ownership of the land or lead to the loss of exploitive possibilities in industry and finance. What they wanted was simply a Nationalist movement which would free them from corrupt rule by Peking and foreign domination—they wanted to be left free to tap the wealth of China in their own way. To continue to support the Kuomintang therefore would mean that the Communists would have to oppose the peasant movement—oppose the very revolution they preached. And, in fact, Moscow issued explicit orders requiring the Chinese Communist Party to bend every effort to prevent peasant uprisings.

Chiang Kai-shek and the right wing of the Kuomintang, on the other hand, could not believe that the peasant disorders which threatened their land ownership and financial interests were not

". . . foreign investment in China was extremely heavy." The imposing banks and commercial buildings on Shanghai's Bund, foreign-owned and managed, dominated China's commerce for decades.

Communist-inspired. Furthermore, Chiang Kai-shek was facing a much more dangerous problem as his forces advanced farther to the north. The European powers were convinced that the Kuomintang was nothing more than a Communist-front organization. A Kuomintang victory would not only rob them of their special privileges and "rights" under the oppressive nineteenth-century treaties: it might lead to a complete overturn of Chinese society which would preclude even an indirect financial exploitation of the country. And foreign investment in China was extremely heavy. As Kuomintang forces approached Shanghai, Chiang Kai-shek had good reason to fear that the foreign troops there (they had been increased to about sixteen thousand men) might enter the fight against him.

For a final complication there was Japan. The Japanese militarists, always anxious to keep China subservient and divided, had made a practice of supporting the warlord regime in Peking. The advance of Kuomintang armies toward Peking heralded a day when China would no longer be exploitable. Therefore, Japanese forces placed themselves in the Kuomintang's way—there were clashes on a local scale, and any further progress might very well bring full-scale Japanese intervention. The prime factor in preventing this was the European imperialist powers' jealousy of Japanese encroachment on their own investments in China. But if Chiang angered the Europeans, then they might support Japan, or at least give her a free hand to "bring order" to China.

The problems were intricate and policy was divided. Borodin and the Russians, although they mistrusted Chiang Kai-shek, decided to gamble on their ability to control him and, during 1926, continued to give him all-out support. The Chinese Communist Party was split—some insisted on continuing the policy of support for the Kuomintang, while others were in favor of doing away with Chiang and attempting to seize control of the revolution themselves. And within the Kuomintang itself there was a split—the left wing favored continued cooperation with the Communists and a continued advance on Peking and Shanghai, while the right wing favored the arrest of Communist leaders and the suppression of the Communist Party accompanied by assurances to the European powers that their rights would be respected. Over the protest of some members, the Chinese Communist Party decided to continue their collaboration with the Kuomintang and their support for Chiang. But as 1927 dawned, both Borodin and the Chinese Communists were preparing to discard Chiang. Meanwhile, Chiang himself had reached certain decisions.

In March of 1927, with Kuomintang forces only twenty-five miles from Shanghai, the workers of the city rose up in rebellion against the local warlord. They were organized and led by Communists, and the uprising was intended to pave the way for Chiang's conquest of the city. But Chiang Kai-shek did not trust the leadership of the Shanghai uprising, and in any event was already in contact with Chinese bankers, foreign diplomats—especially the Japanese consul—and certain secret societies within the city. All agreed that the moment was opportune to have done with the Communists. Accordingly, the police of Shanghai's French settlement opened negotiations between Kuomintang officials and the leaders of the "Green Society"—a semicriminal gang engaged in opium smuggling. In return for large financial rewards, five thousand rifles, and free passage through the foreign settlements, the Green Society agreed to smash the workers' rebellion.

Success was immediate and overwhelming for the Green Society gangs. Caught totally by surprise, the Shanghai workers were slaughtered by the thousands. Chiang Kai-shek himself arrived in Shanghai on March 26, and by April 12 the city was completely in his hands and the local Communist leadership and their mass following had been destroyed.

Nor was anti-Communist action limited to Shanghai. Kuomintang units throughout southern China arrested or killed those suspected of Communist sympathies and stamped out local peasant uprisings everywhere. By July, 1927, Borodin and his staff of Soviet advisers were on their way back to Russia, their policy in ruins. Chiang Kai-shek, now master of all of southern China, established his new capital in Nanking. The new government expelled the Communists from its ranks and waged a ruthless war against its former allies throughout China.

This sudden break with the Communists reflected Chiang Kai-shek's decision to halt the revolution before it remade the life of China—before it transferred land to the peasants and dispossessed the rich. It also reflected his decision to seek foreign backing and recognition, thereby strengthening his movement and forestalling any potential Japanese intervention against it. Among the Communists, their sudden defeat reflected faulty decisions—sometimes made for them many thousands of miles from the scene of action in

Moscow; weak leadership; and the lack of a truly comprehensive program based on the realities of Chinese life. Nor had they yet learned their lesson—as the bloody fiasco of the "Canton Commune" was to dramatically indicate.

In December, 1927, the situation in the city of Canton appeared to the local Communist committees to be ripe for a successful rebellion. Besides being in positions of leadership among the city's trade unions, Communists had also infiltrated a training regiment stationed in Canton. Furthermore, they expected local uprisings in the countryside around the city to distract Kuomintang and local warlord attention. That they were not alone in their hopes was demonstrated by the hearty concurrence of Moscow in their plans—in the eyes of Stalin and his advisers thousands of miles away, the attempt at Canton seemed to mark a new wave of revolutionary activity. Plans were prepared with great thoroughness—but with insufficient secrecy. Canton's chief of police learned something of the conspiracy and began arresting Communist labor leaders wholesale.

The insurrection itself was set for 3:30 A.M. on December 11, 1927. At that hour special Communist assault squads, riding in trucks supplied by the transport workers' union, raced through the dark streets of Canton. Revolutionary headquarters were established in the Russian consulate. Shooting soon broke out as Red Guards and rebellious cadets from the training regiment seized local police stations, post offices, telegraph stations, and barracks. By noon on December 11, the city was in Communist hands and many anti-Communists had been shot. Immediately, a soviet (council) of workers' and soldiers' deputies was chosen to govern the city.

But Communist hopes were premature to say the least. The peasant uprisings outside Canton which were to divert Kuomintang and warlord troops were weak and scattered. Furthermore, through the chief of police, Kuomintang commanders in the field had been alerted that something was afoot. Within two days of the Communist seizure, Kuomintang army units were marching into Canton. Their entry was so sudden and unexpected that resistance had no time to gather. Communist leaders and the rank and file (including officials of the Russian consulate) were speedily rounded up and executed.

During the time of the insurrection, Communists had worn red ties and red scarves to identify themselves. Now that Kuomintang troops were in control they discarded their ties and scarves. But the weather had been extremely hot, and as the wearers perspired, the red dye had discolored their necks. These telltale red stains would not wipe off. Now Kuomintang execution squads roamed the streets, and on finding a suspect, they would examine his neck. If it bore a red stain they thrust a revolver into his mouth and blew his brains out. The killing was indiscriminate and furious; when Kuomintang soldiers realized that they need not waste precious ammunition in machine-gunning their victims, they herded them into boats and took them out onto the river, where they were pushed overboard in lots of ten and twelve, tied together. The massacre continued for nearly a week, during which time more than six thousand people—allegedly Communists—lost their lives in Canton.

Satisfied now that he was in absolute control of the Kuomintang and that Communist opposition had finally been liquidated, Chiang Kai-shek resumed the northward march of his armies from the Yangtze to Peking. The ancient capital fell to Chiang's forces in June, 1928. Renamed Peiping (Northern Peace) by the victorious Chiang, its capture prompted foreign governments throughout the world to grant official recognition to the new Nationalist government of China.

But Chiang had no intention of ruling from the old Manchu capital. Instead he based his new government in Nanking, where imposing new government office buildings soon sprouted. It was to Nanking that Chiang Kai-shek brought the corpse of Sun Yat-sen to be reinterred in a magnificent and imposing marble mausoleum, which was to be a national shrine. But there were many throughout China who thought that Chiang Kai-shek buried Sun Yat-sen's principles along with his body. When Sun died he had observed that

"It was to Nanking that Chiang Kai-shek brought the corpse of Sun Yat-sen to be reinterred in a magnificent and imposing marble mausoleum. . . ."

"the revolution is not yet finished." Now, three years later, in spite of the Kuomintang victory throughout China, that observation remained essentially true. Chiang Kai-shek was about to learn that a revolution cannot be halted at will, cannot be ended at the convenience of, or by the simple decree of, its leadership. The lesson was to be long, terribly costly, and taught in blood.

6

The Long March
into History

In the year 1906, a young peasant from the province of Hunan was standing outside the provincial school at which he was a student. Noticing many bean merchants passing down the road from the city of Changsha, the student asked them why they were fleeing their native city. The merchants explained that there had been a serious famine that year in Changsha and the people were starving. In their misery the people had sent a delegation to the Manchu provincial governor begging for food, but the governor had replied: "Why haven't you anything to eat? The city is full of food. I always have enough." The starving people were enraged by the governor's reply. They attacked the Manchu garrison and threw the governor out of the city. A delegate from the Emperor arrived and promised that things would now be put right. But when a new governor arrived in Changsha he immediately arrested the leaders of the rebellion, beheaded them, and placed their heads on pikes as an example to future rebels. The uprising was crushed.

The young peasant student to whom the bean merchants told their story was Mao Tse-tung—and the vision of what peasants could do when properly led and organized was impressed on his mind thereafter.

Mao was born in 1893 in the village of Shao Shan, in Hunan Province, just south of the great port of Hankow on the Yangtze River. His father, Mao Jen-sheng, was an ex-soldier who had inherited a small farm but later lost it through debt. Nevertheless, by extremely hard work and great frugality, he managed over the years slowly to buy back his land and even add to it until, with three and one-half acres, he qualified as a "rich" peasant in his local village. But the struggle was long and succeeded only because of the old man's ruthless exploitation of his children's labor (he had three sons, of whom Mao was the eldest). Mao's father ruled his family like a Confucian tyrant; he beat his sons regularly, worked them long hours in the fields, kept their mother cowed, and maintained the entire family on near-starvation rations—all the while reciting endless wise proverbs to them about the obedience due from children to their elders. Mao (with his mother's secret encouragement) rebelled, running away from home on several occasions and once, when he was thirteen years old, threatening to commit suicide (which would have disgraced his father in village eyes) to win some measure of freedom.

Yet the old man's tyranny and miserliness accomplished its purpose—he amassed enough money to allow Mao and his brothers to attend local schools while other peasant children of the village remained illiterate. But while young Mao was studying at the local schools and working his father's fields, his education was not only scholastic. From his earliest days he listened eagerly to the tales told by the village elders of their part in the great Taiping Rebellion, and when he learned to read, he devoured the old Chinese romantic classics (such as *All Men Are Brothers* and *The Romance of the Three Kingdoms* with their heroic rebels and legendary Robin Hood-style bandits who fought to help the people) as well as more classical texts.

During the revolution of 1911, Mao spent a few months in Sun Yat-sen's army helping to fight for the republic. His pay was seven dollars a month. He quickly became a teacher to the illiterate peasants of his regiment. But when, in 1912, Yuan Shih-kai seized control of the 1911 revolution and became the republic's first President, Mao quit the army. By then he had witnessed famines, rebellions, executions, and banditry. He had seen for himself something of the strengths and weaknesses of peasant uprisings.

When he left the army, Mao studied the advertisements of the many little colleges which had sprung up in the wake of the revolution—he even tried some of them, including a law school, a commercial school, and an institute of secondary studies. Finally he decided to become a teacher and in 1913 entered the Hunan Normal School, located in Changsha. There he supplemented his studies by spending endless hours in the Changsha library, studying the works of such Western philosophers as John Stuart Mill, Darwin, Rousseau, Spencer, and Montesquieu. He spent his summers tramping through the Hunan countryside with a few friends, studying peasant conditions at first hand. At the Normal School he learned the ancient Chinese classics and became proficient in writing classical poetry. His marks in social sciences were high, but in physical sciences relatively low. It was while studying at Hunan that Mao formed the New People's Study Society—a group of friends who met to discuss philosophy and world affairs and who subjected themselves to a rigorous discipline of winter swimming, marches in the snow, and physical training.

In 1918, his studies at Hunan Normal School completed, Mao went to Peking as a delegate from his New People's Study Society to a congress of such groups being held in the national capital. Mao was twenty-five. He got a job as an assistant librarian at the Peking University library. There he fell in love with the head librarian's daughter, Yang Kai-hui, whom he married in 1920. Later, when Chiang Kai-shek decided to break with and suppress the Chinese Communist Party, Mao's wife was to be murdered by Kuomintang forces.

At Peking, Mao first discovered Communism. He read the *Communist Manifesto* by Marx and Engels, the *Class Struggle* by Kautsky, and Kirkup's *History of Socialism*. By the summer of 1920, Mao considered himself a Marxist; a year later he was one of the dozen men who met at the girls' boarding school in Shanghai to found the Chinese Communist Party.

During the period of Nationalist-Communist collaboration, from 1921 to 1927, Mao generally supported the party line, but with a significant divergence. While he agreed that the Communist Party must collaborate with the middle-class Kuomintang and work with Chiang Kai-shek to achieve unity and freedom, Mao urged that the Communists seek out massive peasant support. Remembering the experiences of his childhood, Mao urged that the Chinese peasantry was a truly revolutionary force and ought to be harnessed to Communist aims. But the Central Committee of the party, in agreement with directives from Moscow, held that only the big-city proletariat (working class) was educated and cohesive enough to form the backbone of a Communist movement. And since this class numbered not more than three million, dependence on the middle-class Kuomintang was a continuing necessity. Mao did not completely disagree with this thesis—he simply wanted to organize mass support among the peasantry as a sort of insurance against possible betrayal by the Kuomintang. However, although he was a member of the Central Committee, Mao's position was subordinate and his views were not heeded.

In February of 1927, Mao undertook a field trip through his native province of Hunan to study peasant conditions. As a result he wrote a report for the Communist Party Central Committee entitled *Report on an Investigation into the Peasant Movement in Hunan*. In this remarkable document Mao stated that the Chinese peasantry was on the verge of revolution. They would soon "rise like a tornado." Furthermore, it was the overwhelming mass of the poorest peasants who were taking the initiative in forming associations and semisecret societies. The entire countryside was aflame. Either the Communist Party would place itself at the head of this incipient peasant revolution or it would suffer a bloody defeat. Those party comrades who bothered to read Mao's report sneered. Classical Marxist dogma taught that only the working class could lead a revolution—the activities of the peasants were formless, pointless, and ought to be suppressed because they alarmed the landlords of the Kuomintang with whom the Communists were allied.

A few weeks later, in the bloody streets of Shanghai, the Kuomintang gave its answer to Communist hopes of collaboration. But even this did not teach the party leadership the error of its ways. The abortive and terribly costly Canton uprising was not sufficient either —lesser but equally hopeless uprisings continued to take place in various cities during 1927, even after the Communist Party had been driven underground. But in the meantime, Mao, without authority from the Central Committee, had returned to Hunan. There he gathered together peasant support and, in late August, 1927, launched a revolt which became known as the Autumn Harvest Uprising. By September the successful peasants had organized what they were pleased to call the First Division of the First Peasants and Workers Army. Joining them were worker refugees from the bloody disasters at Canton and Shanghai, some local miners, and even a few brigades of Chiang Kai-shek's Kuomintang troops.

But the First Division was badly armed and totally inexperienced. It was soon surrounded by Chiang Kai-shek's forces and driven into retreat. Mao himself was captured by Kuomintang troops—and nearly beheaded. While he was being led to his execution he suddenly broke away from his captors and fled into a nearby swamp. Moving only by night, and heading south, Mao emerged from the swamp barefoot and with only seven dollars in his pocket, a fugitive. But local peasants befriended him and led him back to the remnants of his troops. With about one thousand of these he retreated to a nearly impregnable mountain fastness called Chingkangshan, "Mountain of Wells and Ridges." There, from defeat and disaster in other parts of China, Communist units and Communist leaders slowly arrived during the following months. But the Central Committee of the Communist Party took the occasion to repudiate Mao. He was expelled from the Central Committee and viewed with distaste and suspicion by both Moscow and the doctrinaire Chinese Communist leadership. Nonetheless, he imperturbably continued along his chosen path. In November, 1927, Mao organized the first Chinese soviet—in the town of Tsalin in Hunan.

Among the reinforcements who joined Mao at Tsalin were Chu Teh and Chou En-lai, two men who had traveled vastly different paths to get there.

Chu Teh (whose name means "Red Virtue") had been born into a family of rich landowners in 1886. Given an excellent education, he was a highly cultured youth, well versed in the classics. At the age of twenty he became a soldier, joined the Sun Yat-sen forces, and fought well against the Manchu armies in 1911. When the 1911 revolution ran into the sands he left the army to become a high government official in the province of Yunnan. There he fell victim to the opium-smoking habit. But he continued his reading, and when he reflected on the disasters which were overwhelming his country, he had a bad conscience. Accordingly, in 1922 he gave up his post, bade good-bye to his wife and family, packed a suitcase, and boarded a boat bound for Europe—on which he knew he would not find a single grain of opium. He suffered terribly during this enforced "cure," but awoke one morning with no desire for the "pipe." He visited France and Germany and Russia. In Moscow he attended the University of the Toilers of the East, where he studied Marxism and military tactics. Returning to China in 1925, he appeared in Shanghai, was given command of certain Communist provincial

Chu Teh

forces, and, after the Kuomintang offensive against their former allies, retreated with the fragments of his command to Hunan to find sanctuary in Mao's soviet.

Chou En-lai was born in 1898, the son of a well-to-do family of scholar-intellectuals. His grandfather had been a mandarin, a high official at the Manchu court; his father a university professor. Chou himself had a thorough education which was interrupted by a year spent in prison as one of the leaders of the May 4 movement in 1919. On being released from jail, Chou went to France, where he spent four years studying Western institutions, organizing Chinese overseas groups to support the Communist Party, traveling in Germany, and supporting himself with such jobs as dishwashing. On his return to China in 1924 he was appointed political instructor at the new Whampoa Military Academy (of which Chiang Kai-shek was the director). Chiang dispatched Chou in 1925 to Shanghai. There he

Chou En-lai

was to organize the workers in preparation for the Nationalist conquest of that city. Chou En-lai succeeded admirably in this task—only to see his men slaughtered by Kuomintang-supported gangsters in April of 1927. He escaped from that debacle with a price on his head and made his way to Canton. But with the bloody suppression of the Canton commune a few months later, Chou had once more to flee—this time as part of Chu Teh's retreating forces, of which he was appointed political commissar.

With these reinforcements and others which continually trickled into his base on the Mountain of Wells and Ridges, Mao began to extend the area of his soviet. He had arrived at an interpretation of the situation which he issued in 1928 under the title "How Can China's Red Power Exist?" In this essay Mao demonstrated that a revolutionary army must be founded on a broad territorial base. This required that the inhabitants of these territories share in both the work and the benefits of Communist rule. Land must be given to the peasants, and, in turn, peasants must be enlisted into the Red Army as volunteers. Three principles of behavior were promulgated in the Red Army: obedience to orders, no confiscation whatsoever from the poor peasants, and prompt delivery to the government of anything taken from the landlords. Eight further rules of behavior were made into a song to be remembered by all troops:

1. Replace doors when you leave a house. (The wooden peg-hung doors of Chinese peasant houses serve admirably as beds.)
2. Return and roll up the straw matting (used for sleeping on and under).
3. Be courteous and polite to the people and help them.
4. Return all borrowed articles.
5. Replace all damaged articles.
6. Be honest in all transactions with the peasants.
7. Pay for all articles purchased.
8. Be sanitary—build latrines at a safe distance from people's houses.

These rules were a revolution in Chinese military conduct. For thousands of years the soldier had been dreaded and hated by the peasant, and soldiers' conduct had been a long story of rape, plunder, and murder. But here was a new kind of army—an army that helped the peasants plant their grain and helped them harvest it; an army which did not rob them but on the contrary taught them how to improve their native villages; an army which took the land from landlords and gave it to the people; an army which, instead of marching off the young men at gun point for military service, asked them to volunteer to defend a common cause. Furthermore, this was an army which fought well and was led by officers who cared so much for the well-being of their men that they taught them to read and write. Truly a unique army in the Chinese experience!

An ancient Chinese sage said: "The people are the water and the

Imperial government floats atop the water." But Mao Tse-tung said: "The people are the water and we are the fishes who swim in the water." Only a complete consolidation of people and army could, he knew, lead to victory or even survival. The tactics and strategy of army operations were founded on this simple precept. Lacking arms and outnumbered many times over, China's new Red Army would have to fight in partisan fashion, seeking protection among the people and emerging from them. Four simple tactical slogans were evolved and repeated endlessly until every soldier understood them:

When the enemy advances, we retreat.
When the enemy halts and encamps, we trouble him.
When the enemy seeks to avoid battle, we attack.
When the enemy retreats, we pursue.

By 1930, Mao's policy was so successful that the Communists controlled fifteen "liberated regions," of which Kiangsi Province was the center. The Red Army comprised sixty thousand "regulars" and could count on the support of fifty million peasants.

Chiang Kai-shek decided that the time had come to liquidate this menace. Between 1930 and 1935 he launched five campaigns against the Red Army areas. Each was heralded, with much fanfare, as a "Final Extermination Campaign"—and the first four failed disastrously. Time and again Kuomintang troops refused to fight against Red forces—on one occasion, in 1931, a large part of the Kuomintang's 26th Army went over *en masse* to the Communist side. It was from repeated campaigns against Kuomintang forces that Mao's soldiers captured the arms and ammunition which sustained them.

In 1934 Chiang Kai-shek threw nearly one million men into his fifth "Final Extermination Campaign" against Mao's forces. This time he employed new tactics. Under the advice of German generals von Seekt and Falkenhausen, Kuomintang forces, instead of rushing into prepared traps, advanced very slowly, building up stone fortresses over the countryside, removing the civilian peasant populations from vast areas, improving communications, and gradually closing a ring of steel around the Red Army.

Mao Tse-tung might possibly have held Kiangsi Province had his views prevailed. But while Mao was chairman of the committees in the liberated areas, he was subordinate to the wishes of the Central Committee of the Chinese Communist Party. The men on that committee, for the most part, still clung to the old idea that city workers must lead the revolution. Therefore, when Chiang Kai-shek's forces advanced into the "liberated areas," the committee insisted on fighting positional battles to hold on to towns and cities. Over 180,000 Red Army men were thrown into such hopeless battles, completely reversing Mao's partisan strategy. Inevitably the Red Army lost. It was only after suffering all but complete catastrophe that the Central Committee decided to leave control of the remains of the Red Army and its much-shrunken base of operations to Mao Tse-tung. By now the position had become all but hopeless. With forces reduced to no more than ninety thousand men (against Kuomintang forces estimated at half a million), with the enemy almost completely encircling them, Mao's men had to face surrender—or retreat. Retreat would have to be speedy, secret, and in itself a running battle. Mao decided upon retreat. On October 16, 1934, with what equipment and supplies they could carry with them, the Red Army abandoned its hard-won soviet in Kiangsi Province and started out on a great strategic retreat which became known as the Long March.

In Chinese, Long March is translated as *Chang Cheng*. But the word *Chang* also invokes a meaning of immortality. The fabulous march upon which Mao's Red Army now embarked was one of the greatest in history—comparable only to the march of Xenophon's ten thousand Greeks as recorded in the *Anabasis*. The main route was to cover more than six thousand miles; but with all the twists and turns, tactical backtracking, and circumventions, very many units were to travel more than twice that distance. It was to be one of the great triumphs of men against odds and over nature.

The weakest link in the Kuomintang encirclement lay in the west in Kweichow Province. There local warlords cooperating with Chiang Kai-shek could not prevent the Red Army from breaking through. The Reds captured the local administrative town of Tsunyi, and there, in January of 1935, a conference of the Central Committee of the Chinese Communist Party acknowledged Mao Tse-tung as its leader. Mao became Chairman of the Central Committee, while those whose advice had led to the disasters of the previous years stepped down and were replaced by Mao's followers. But Tsunyi was only a stopover on the continuing retreat.

The first obstacle beyond Kweichow was the crossing of the upper Yangtze, the "Gold Sand" River. In western Yunnan Province, where the Red Army intended to make their crossing, the Yangtze runs swiftly through deep mountain gorges. The very few bridges across the torrent were occupied by Kuomintang troops and all the ferryboats had been withdrawn to the north bank. Chiang Kai-shek intended to destroy the Red Army in this mountainous region. Mao Tse-tung ordered a four-day forced march, which brought his forces to within a few miles of Kunming, the provincial capital city. Chiang, imagining that the Reds would seize the place as they had seized Tsunyi, rushed his forces ahead to occupy it. But the Red threat was only a diversion; their main columns traveled by night northwestward toward the great bend of the Yangtze, where one of the few navigable points on the upper river was located. On the way the Red Army captured a Kuomintang messenger. He was carrying orders to officials at the crossing to burn all the boats. But the Reds treated the messenger well and won him over to their cause. Thereupon he led one of their columns to the crossing. When they arrived they found only one boat remaining on the river bank—and it could carry only ten men at a time and took about forty minutes to make a round trip. The first party of Red soldiers dressed in captured Kuomintang uniforms, crossed over, and talked the officials on the northern bank into sending boats back for their comrades. Eight more boats were rounded up, but even so it took the army eight days and nights to complete their crossing of the Gold Sand River.

Beyond the upper Yangtze, in western Szechwan Province, there was yet another strategic river to cross—the Tatu. It twisted through mountainous defiles and gorges thousands of feet deep. It was here that the heroes of Mao's favorite classical romance, *The Romance of the Three Kingdoms*, had met defeat and here also that the last of the Taiping rebel armies, 100,000 strong, had been massacred by the Imperial Manchu armies. Mao and Chu Teh had studied both of those campaigns and knew them by heart. They realized that the main cause for the former defeats had been unnecessary delay. To avoid a similar fate they had to beat Chiang Kai-shek's pursuing

forces to the river. The only way to accomplish this was to march through the forbidding forest region which was occupied by an aboriginal tribe called Lolos. The Lolos hated all Chinese, and with good reason, for they had been persecuted by Imperial forces since time immemorial. But Mao sent one of his officers who spoke the aboriginal Lolo language to explain to these fierce tribesmen that this Chinese army was different—it was fighting against the Lolos' traditional enemies and its principles included recognition of the rights of primitive peoples. The Lolos were won over and the Red Army passed through their territory without incident—a feat which

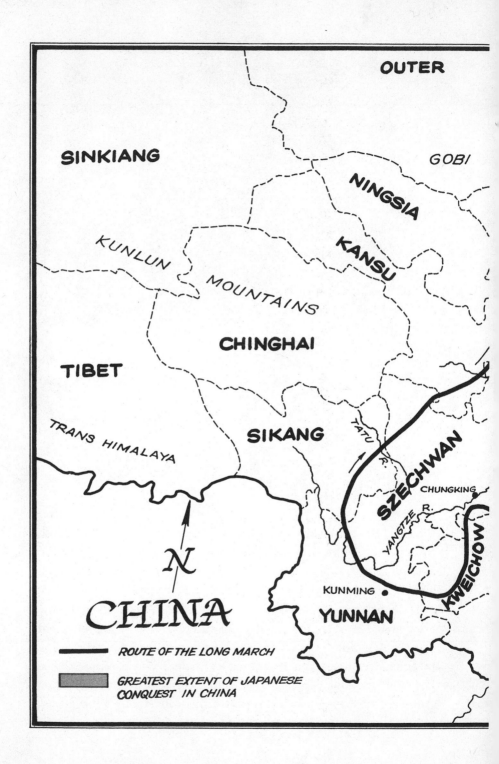

SINKIANG

OUTER

GOBI

NINGSIA

KANSU

KUNLUN MOUNTAINS

CHINGHAI

TIBET

SIKANG

TRANS HIMALAYA

TATU R.

SZECHWAN

CHUNGKING

YANGTZE R.

N

CHINA

KWEICHOW

KUNMING

YUNNAN

ROUTE OF THE LONG MARCH

GREATEST EXTENT OF JAPANESE
CONQUEST IN CHINA

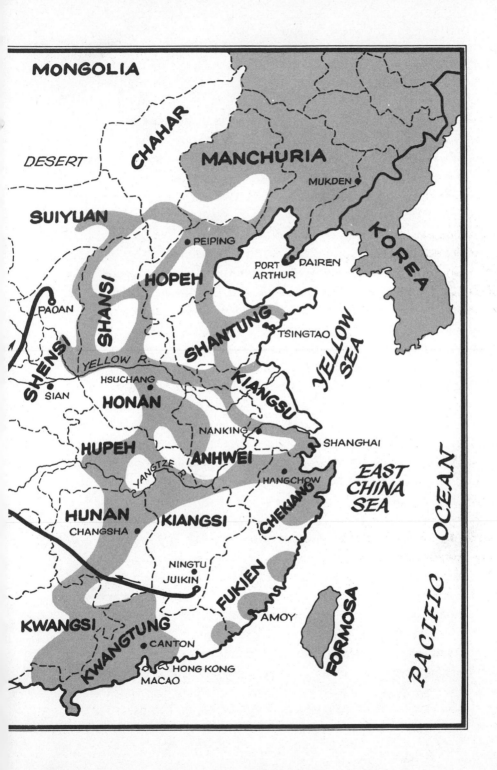

MONGOLIA

DESERT

CHAHAR

MANCHURIA

SUIYUAN

MUKDEN

PEIPING

HOPEH

SHANSI

PAOAN

PORT DAIREN
ARTHUR

KOREA

SHENSI

YELLOW R.

SHANTUNG

TSINGTAO

YELLOW
SEA

HSUCHANG

KIANGSU

SIAN

HONAN

NANKING

SHANGHAI

HUPEH

ANHWEI

EAST
CHINA
SEA

YANGTZE R.

HANGCHOW

HUNAN

KIANGSI

CHEKIANG

CHANGSHA

NINGTU

JUIKIN

FUKIEN

KWANGSI

KWANGTUNG

AMOY

FORMOSA

PACIFIC OCEAN

CANTON

HONG KONG

MACAO

would have been utterly impossible for the men of Chiang Kai-shek.

However, when the Red Army reached the nearest ferryboat crossing, surprising and capturing the small local garrison, they found that there were only four boats and the crossing was so slow and difficult that it would take more than a month to ferry the army over the river. So they continued their march along the river banks and up into the mountains toward the last bridge over the river, the Luting Bridge. The Luting Bridge was a structure of twelve heavy chains which supported wooden planks. It stretched between two mountains over a chasm thousands of feet deep through which the Tatu River rushed in a white-foam torrent. When they reached this precarious bridge, the Red Army found that the boards had been removed—only the twelve iron chains swayed in the wind over the gorge. Furthermore, on the opposite side, in the village of Luting, enemy forces covered the bridge approaches with gun fire.

Under cover of the massed fire of their comrades, twenty-two men, led by a company commander named Liao, made their way hand-over-hand across the iron chains, in the teeth of heavy enemy fire. Each man carried a Tommy gun, a broad sword, and twelve hand grenades, which they used as best they could while trying to hang on to the chains. Behind them came another company of troops who laid new planks on the bridge. When the first group reached the far side, a great wall of fire arose at the bridgehead: the enemy was trying to burn the chain supports. The assault squad hesitated only for a moment and then plunged into the fire to fight their way into the village of Luting. They were soon followed by other forces and at last both bridge and village were secured. The assault squad was ever afterward to become legendary as the Twenty-Two Heroes of Tatu. The main army was now free to make its way to the northwest.

Ahead of Mao's men lay range after range of high, snow-capped mountains. They marched for four hours and rested for four hours, making twenty-four miles on an average day. As the passes through the mountains grew higher and higher, blinding snowstorms stung their faces as they trudged over treacherous ice. The pass over the

Great Snowy Mountain was sixteen thousand feet above sea level. Later, Mao was to recall: "On Pao-tung Kang peak alone one army lost two-thirds of its transport animals. Hundreds fell down and never got up again." Frostbite cases became common—and there were almost no medical supplies with which to treat them. Amputations were often performed in mid-march and without anesthetic. But at last, in July, those who survived this incredible trek emerged into eastern Tibet. However, their trials were far from ended.

Pushing ever northward, the Red Army advanced now into wild regions inhabited by warring tribesmen who fought them every step of the way. These wild aboriginals could not be reached by reason or negotiation—they were completely indifferent to Communist proclamations of equality for national minorities. The land they inhabited—steaming jungles, dank forests, quicksand-filled marshes —offered perfect cover for ambushes and surprise attacks. The Red Army lost many men in these wild regions. For weeks, Mao recalled, it cost the life of one soldier for every sheep they could capture to feed the starving forces.

Early in the fall the Red Army emerged from this dreadful area into the eery region known as the Great Grasslands. These were actually high swamps covered by seas of floating grass, and a perpetual rain fell upon them. The army marched for days at a time without ever spotting a single human habitation. The only way through these treacherous bogs, into which hundreds of men sank forever, was a maze of narrow footpaths known only to the very few inhabitants of the region, and these had to be captured before they would lead the Red forces through. Even with this enforced help their passage was a terrible one. There was no dry wood for fuel, nothing but herbs and roots to eat, no drinking water to be found, not even any trees for shade from the fierce sun. By the time they emerged from the Great Grasslands into the Kansu plain, the Red Army had been reduced to seven thousand men.

Now, as they approached the northwest, Mao's men were entering Chinese Moslem territory. The Moslems of China, fierce and fanatical, had maintained intermittent warfare against Chinese governments for centuries in protection of their rights and native customs. Nor, with their deeply religious way of life, were they amenable to Communist propaganda. If the Moslems of the northwest were not to fall *en masse* on Mao's weakened troops, they would have to be won over by man-to-man contact and by personal examples of good conduct on the part of the troops. Mao issued a set of rules:

1. Mosques and priests must be protected. Do not enter Holy Places. Do not stick posters on the sides of mosques.
2. Never eat pork, horse, or mule in a Moslem house.
3. Leave Moslem women alone and never enter their houses.
4. Do not interrupt religious services.
5. Do not use Moslem baths.
6. Wash your hands before taking water from a Moslem well and never throw water back into the well.
7. Call the Moslems "Old Compatriots" or "Old Cousins," but never use any term of disrespect toward them.
8. Never mention pigs in front of a Moslem. Never ask them why they do not eat pork or what goes on in their mosques.
9. Never drink or smoke in a Moslem house.
10. Explain to everyone the party's policy regarding national minorities.

These new and practical Ten Commandments were not entirely successful. Some Moslem leaders resisted the Red Army passage through their territories. There were skirmishes against Moslem cavalry. But the conduct of Mao's troops was so exemplary that in general the Moslems did not oppose their march and even, on occasion, aided them. On October 25, 1935, the Red Army reached its goal—Shensi Province far in the northwest of China. There they established a temporary headquarters at the village of Paoan which was later moved to the city of Yenan, and looked back on what they had accomplished.

They had marched three hundred and sixty-eight days, crossed eighteen mountain ranges, forded twenty-four rivers, fought a skirmish somewhere along the line once a day, and fought fifteen major battles. They had passed through twelve provinces and eluded, tricked, or defeated Kuomintang armies numbering three hundred thousand men, while breaking through the local forces of ten different warlords. They had marched through aboriginal territories in which no Chinese army had been seen for centuries. Their accomplishment of making a six-thousand-mile retreat and arriving with morale as high as or higher than when they had started almost makes Hannibal's crossing of the Alps and Napoleon's Russian campaigns seem like summer picnics.

Furthermore, there was a deep and serious purpose in marching to Shensi. For here the Red forces were within easy reach of the Mongolian border and the Soviet Union. From here they could advance toward Peking and Manchuria and down the rich Yellow River basin, and to this remote area Chiang Kai-shek would have difficulty sending any more armies on "Final Extermination Campaigns." To Shensi now came scattered Red units from various regions of the northwest to unite with Mao's decimated forces and found a new soviet.

Mao Tse-tung wrote a poem to commemorate this incredible march, and it was translated by the American journalist Edgar Snow, who visited him in Paoan soon after the Red Army's arrival there:

The Red Army, never fearing the challenging Long March,
Looked lightly on the many peaks and rivers,
Wu Meng's range rose, lowered, rippled,
And green-tiered were the rounded steps of Wu Meng.
Warm-beating the Gold Sand River's waves against the rocks,
And cold the iron chain spans of Tatu bridge.
A thousand joyous li of freshening snow on Min Shan,
And then, the last pass vanquished, the Armies smiled.

7

Nationalist China and Japanese Aggression

WHILE CHIANG Kai-shek's armies were waging their "Final Extermination Campaigns" and the Red Army was making its long trek to the northwest provinces, the Nationalist government, based at Nanking, had an opportunity to start building the kind of China they wanted. Very shortly Japanese invasion and the advent of World War II were to interrupt and disrupt their programs—but from 1928 until 1936, the ideas of Chiang Kai-shek and his followers were to find expression in the kind of government—or lack of it—which arose throughout that part (and it was by far the largest part) of China under their control.

The principles of Chiang's Kuomintang Party had originally been established by Sun Yat-sen. Thus, when Chiang achieved power in 1928-1929, he followed Sun's design for a new government. The Nationalist regime was to be divided into five agencies (*yuan*): executive, legislative, judicial, civil service, and censorial. Within the executive yuan were to be found ministries for foreign affairs, war, communications, etc. The civil service (examination) yuan and the censorial (control) yuan were derived from older Imperial traditions. The control yuan soon developed into an all-powerful secret police agency which, in truly eclectic fashion, found itself copying the methods of the German Gestapo, the Russian OGPU, and the Tokyo Municipal Police Department.

Sun Yat-sen had also developed the theory of a revolution in three stages—military unification, political tutelage, and, finally, political democracy. This found expression in the Nationalist announcement in 1928 that the period of military unification was completed and now China was to enter the period of political tutelage under a Kuomintang dictatorship.

The Nationalist government in Nanking was established by the Kuomintang and was legally responsible only to the Kuomintang—not to the people. The political rights of the people, including the right to elect representatives, were to be held "in custody" for the people by the all-powerful party, which in turn was to "instruct" the people in their proper use. In actuality, no such instruction ever took place. The Nationalist government remained a one-party dictatorship and quickly fell prey to the corruption, ruthlessness, and chauvinism which absolute power engenders. More than that, it fell increasingly under the absolute domination of its leader, Chiang Kai-shek. No matter what his title of the moment might be (and he was at various times "Generalissimo," Party Secretary, Chairman, and once even "retired"), real power remained with Chiang Kai-shek.

The one-man rule of the Generalissimo (as his followers now styled him) was not simply the reflections of personal ambition; it did have objective roots. The Nationalists had come to power through military revolution. The suppression of warlord armies and defense against foreign encroachments had made a military leadership inevitable. On the military level only a "strong man" could find the power to achieve the first part of the Nationalist program—military unification of the country. Since the Kuomintang Party was dominated (especially after its break with the Communists in 1927) by landlord and business interests, it had to suppress the peasant uprisings and the city workers' unions. Therefore, it could not count on any broadly based mass support for its program and had to depend on the army and the army's leader to maintain itself in power. Over the years, the Kuomintang government came more and more to reflect the ideas and personality of Chiang Kai-shek.

There is no doubt that Chiang sincerely wished to rid his country of foreign domination. He was a fervent patriot within the limits of what he conceived to be possible. In 1928 the Nationalists commenced a "rights recovery movement" aimed at abolishing the unequal treaties which had been imposed upon China during the nineteenth century—and this movement was at least partially successful. At the Washington Conference in 1922, certain modifications in the rights of foreigners in China had been introduced under American pressure. With continued American support, by 1930 Nanking had secured treaties which placed many of the citizens of less powerful foreign countries, such as Holland and Italy, under Chinese legal authority when they lived in China. British, American, French, and Japanese citizens continued, of course, to remain largely outside that authority. Furthermore, the Nationalist regime sought to abolish the special concessions under which foreigners operated in the Treaty Ports. They were at least partially successful in this also—by 1937 the thirty-three concessions leased to foreign governments had been reduced to thirteen. Nor was the Nationalist program of regaining control of China brought to a halt by the resistance of the foreign powers so much as it was by fear of Japanese aggression. Thus the continued presence of British and American warships on Chinese rivers and Anglo-American troops in Chinese cities was looked upon as a means of forestalling Japanese encroachments. The Nationalists considered those foreign concessions and the international settlements which remained at Shanghai and Amoy as a means of keeping Britain and the United States involved in China's fate, thereby deterring the onward march of Japanese imperialism.

The Kuomintang had come to power as a revolutionary organization. The traditions behind it were authoritarian, not democratic. In the long struggle against Manchus, warlords, and foreign imperialists, a premium had been placed upon secrecy, ruthlessness, and the following of orders—not on the unwieldy processes of popular democratic control. It was perhaps inevitable that when it assumed power the Kuomintang could not shake itself of these old habits. And, like revolutionists in other times and places, the Kuomintang leaders grew more conservative as they grew older. Bureaucratic privileges became increasingly more important to them than practical efficiency; more and more, their regime became simply a defense of their own personal prerogatives and interests. But in this process of "aging revolution" there was also a paramount objective factor. By suppressing the continuance of the revolution by the oppressed peasants and workers, the Kuomintang leadership had cut itself off from its base. Its continued domination of China therefore came more and more to depend on the apparatus of the police state —an apparatus that operated not too differently from the old Manchu Imperial machine.

The basic regeneration of Chinese life had to take place at the village level. Old Hundred Names had to be given some sort of economic security, an education, and political participation in his own destiny. And, in an attempted reorganization of the village political structure, the Kuomintang government did try at least to introduce new political forms into village life. But these forms had no content—they were not, in fact, based on any real change in the power structure of the village; the landlord remained supreme, education was beyond the reach of all but a tiny minority, and political democracy was somehow to be imposed from above rather than to rise from below. A very essential difference between the Kuomintang and the Communist Party dictatorships was the fact that the Kuomintang relied upon the continued support of the landlord in order to maintain itself, while the Communists sought to seize power by opposing the landlords.

The Kuomintang method of government found a theoretical justi-
fication in ancient Confucian doctrine. By 1934, with nothing better
to offer, Chiang Kai-shek started his New Life Movement, an
adaptation of Confucian principles. The New Life Movement instructed the people in moral virtues—such as "proper behavior according to status," "judicious conduct," and "the sense of personal
conscience." In ninety-six rules Chiang sought to organize the life
of the individual much as he might have organized the lives of
cadets in a military academy. The rules included not eating noisily,
walking with correct posture, keeping one's clothes buttoned, nonsmoking, nonspitting, promptness, etc. In a book entitled *China's
Destiny,* published in 1943, Chiang was to expand on the theme of
authority as the basis of life. It was the only philosophical and practical program he could offer.

On a practical level, Kuomintang doctrine led to repression and
futility. The Kuomintang secret police proliferated. Part of their
job was to eradicate "incorrect thinking." The harassment, impris-
onment, and occasional murder of Chinese intellectuals and students became a feature of Chinese life. Such actions were usually
justified by the claim that the victims were Communists—but in
increasing numbers they were not: they were simply individuals
who happened to disagree with the Kuomintang program in one or
another of its doctrines. Nor without the mobilization of the peasants could the Kuomintang achieve anything toward irrigation,
flood control, and the elimination of famine and pestilence. The
Yellow River, the Yangtze, and their tributaries continued to rage
unchecked in predictable floods; famines in which millions of people
perished continued to ravage the countryside—and pestilence followed in immemorial fashion as it had in the days of the earliest
emperors.

In the field of education the Kuomintang program called for the
training of more than 500,000 graduate students—but these were
to be technologists such as engineers, chemists, doctors, architects,
etc. Only a small fraction were to be economists, sociologists, busi-

nessmen. Without taking any steps to establish a groundwork of social and economic reform, a mechanical technocracy was to be brought into being.

Chiang Kai-shek's attitude toward the remnants of the Communist movement and the surviving Red Army in the northwest followed the rigid lines of his military background. Incapable of advancing a program which by raising the living standards, hopes, and aspirations of the Chinese people might have undermined the Communist appeal, he placed total reliance on military means to defend his regime against the Communist threat. This in turn placed greater burdens on the already overburdened people in the form of high taxes, military conscription, and the widespread destruction of civil war. By its emphasis on militarism—on the loyalty of the officers' corps, the organization of vast armies, the subordination of life to military ends—it brought into being a class of officers whose interest it was to preserve the authoritarian nature of the Kuomintang regime. The idea that the Communists had to be physically exterminated and national unity thereby achieved became a growing obsession with Chiang Kai-shek and his followers, until, during the Second World War, American observers were to see it as a mania.

Physically, the Nationalist regime made a good start toward the modernization of China. Railroads were built into the hinterlands, motor roads constructed, telegraph stations established, and airfields developed in a program which, if rudimentary by American standards, was nevertheless extravagant by Chinese standards. Of course, a large part of the impetus for this development was military and doctrinal rather than purely practical. With these new communications Chiang's government was better able to control the coun-

NEXT PAGES: *"The rules included not eating noisily, walking with correct posture, keeping one's clothes buttoned, nonsmoking, nonspitting, promptness, etc."*

tryside and also to wage its continuing civil war against the Communists and, later, a defensive war against the Japanese.

In considering the success and failure of Chiang Kai-shek's Kuomintang regime, it must not be forgotten that whatever its internal failings and contradictions, it was under abnormally heavy pressure from external threats. Thus Chiang Kai-shek, in seeking American and British support against growing Japanese encroachment, had to walk the tightrope of convincing Anglo-American business interests that he was indeed the "strong man" with whom and through whom they could deal to develop their own commercial interests in China, and yet maintain an anti-imperialistic attitude before his own people, who would no longer countenance concessions to foreigners. Furthermore, in his opposition to the Japanese, Chiang, lacking revolutionary mass support among China's millions, had to be extremely careful not to provoke Japan into an all-out war against China. That this policy, no matter how rationalized, was essentially foolish does not alter the fact that China's era of appeasement was only a part of a world-wide policy of appeasement toward European dictators and Japanese militarists practiced by the Western democracies as well as Chiang.

Japan had been steadily encroaching upon China ever since the last decades of the nineteenth century. With a large industrial establishment but almost no raw materials and a home market too small to absorb its industrial output, Japan saw in China (and in fact, all of east Asia) both a source of vital raw materials and a huge market for her surplus production. Only the presence of other powers in China had prevented an earlier Japanese attempt to conquer the country directly. But by 1931, Japanese militarists considered themselves sufficiently strong and European powers and America sufficiently complacent to launch an open attack. Of equal importance in their calculations was the fact that China was at last becoming united. Although warlordism remained, Chiang Kai-shek's Nationalist government had steadily extended its control. In the wake of unity was a small but significant growth of industry. China showed signs of awakening and the Japanese knew that if they were to continue to dominate Asian markets they would have to act quickly.

On September 18, 1931, a rail was torn up on the South Manchuria Railroad (which was owned by Japan but ran through northeast China). The fact that this rail was displaced along a stretch of tracks heavily guarded by Japanese troops and that it was discovered *after* an express train had passed without injury led many observers to conclude that the Japanese had arranged the incident themselves as an excuse. In any case, Japanese troops instantly attacked the city of Mukden, capital of Manchuria (northeast China). Within a few hours they had seized all strategic points in the area. Within a few days they had taken over the principal towns and villages as well. By the end of the month they controlled all of Manchuria—and it was apparent they were there to stay.

Manchuria, although beyond the Great Wall, was an integral part of China. Furthermore, it contained an overwhelmingly large percentage of China's industrial capacity as well as great reserves of raw materials. Like other areas of the country Manchuria had been subject to various warlords—but it was in no sense a non-Chinese region. Indeed, native Chinese comprise ninety-five per cent of its population. After the warlord Chang Tso-lin had been driven from Peking during the Nationalist advance of 1928-1929, he had established his base of power in Manchuria, which he ruled more or less independently of the Nationalist regime in Nanking. But after Chang Tso-lin's assassination at the hands of Japanese officers, he was succeeded by his son, Chang Hsueh-liang. Young Chang had been warned by the Japanese, in no uncertain terms, that it would be a good thing if the northeast did not take part in the unification of China or submit in any way to Chiang Kai-shek's government. Young Chang's response to these threats was to hoist the Nationalist flag in 1929 and acknowledge that Manchuria was indeed part of China. The Japanese attacked two years later.

Japan's sudden move created crisis abroad as well as in China. The old imperialist powers, such as Britain, France, and, to a lesser de-

gree, the United States, now had to reckon with a decided threat to
their commercial interests not only in China but in all of Asia. To
confuse and persuade them, the Japanese advanced three arguments: first they pointed out that unless China were kept in her
place by a foreign domination which Japan was best qualified to
carry out, then that nation's vast millions would unite and "upset
the balance of power," not only throughout Asia, but throughout
the world. Secondly, the Japanese attempted to convince the West
that their primary target was not China, but Soviet Russian Siberia
—and any attack on the Soviet Union ought to be welcomed by the
capitalist democracies. Finally, the Japanese did everything in their
power to advance the fiction that Manchuria was in some way not
really a part of China. They were favored in this lie by the fact that
the region had in fact been under tsarist Russian, Japanese, and local
warlord domination for many years. The Japanese even gave the area
a new name—Manchukuo—and put the former child-emperor Pu
Yi on a puppet throne there. Although it is easy now to see how
ridiculous all these arguments and claims really were, many people
were taken in by them during the 1930's.

In Great Britain, where many wistfully recalled the old Anglo-
Japanese alliance of World War I and where Japan was still looked
upon as a Far Eastern makeweight against Soviet Russian ambitions,
the reaction was one of polite but indifferent regret. The other
European nations, with neither the force nor the will to oppose
Japanese expansion, could not be expected to intervene. Only two
possible sources of help remained to Chiang Kai-shek: the Soviet
Union and the United States. But Chiang had broken relations with
Soviet Russia in 1928, after his brutal suppression of the Chinese
Communist Party in Shanghai and Canton. Although the United
States, in the person of her Secretary of State, Henry L. Stimson,
saw clearly enough that the Japanese were in the process of closing
America's long-cherished "Open Door" in China, and although
many Americans—especially in the navy and war departments—had
long recognized that a clash with Japan was all but inevitable sooner

or later, the overwhelming majority of the American people were isolationist. They did not want to become embroiled in foreign wars, either in Asia or in Europe. Furthermore, the great American military establishment of World War I had been dismantled to the point where the United States stood small chance of success in a war in east Asia. To add to these complications, 1931 was, of course, one of the worst years of the Great Depression which was sweeping Europe and America. The most that Secretary Stimson felt able to do was issue a formal protest to the Japanese government and announce that the United States would not recognize Japanese gains, either by direct conquest or by indirect subversion, in Asia. Britain aligned herself with this policy.

Nonrecognition, however, was as useless to Chiang Kai-shek as it was ineffective in stopping Japanese aggression. The Generalissimo decided to take China's case to the League of Nations. True, neither the United States nor Soviet Russia was a member of the League— but perhaps if sufficient world opinion were mobilized on China's behalf, something effective might be accomplished. The League of Nations sent a commission to Manchuria to "find out what had happened," and received a report which was a masterpiece of diplomatic evasion. Even this self-abasement did not satisfy Japan, which now withdrew from the League of Nations.

The impotence with which the League responded to Japanese expansionism in Asia gave a powerful impetus to the ambitions of the new European dictatorships of Adolf Hitler and Benito Mussolini. It has long been assumed that the League of Nations was wrecked by its failure to contain European fascism: actually it was destroyed earlier by this shameful acquiescence to Japanese imperialism. But Chiang Kai-shek's decision to appeal to the League did in fact serve its purpose in that it brought Japanese intentions out into the open for all to see. Furthermore, he was able to align Great Britain and the United States on his own side, diplomatically if not militarily. Business leaders in both countries now became aware that Japanese expansion was a direct threat to their own interests in China. Nor

"Nor was the Anglo-American public conscience dead. . . ."

was the Anglo-American public conscience dead: a great and politically important wave of sympathy extended to Chiang Kai-shek as the symbol of Chinese resistance to Japan.

Unfortunately, Chiang's resistance remained much more symbolic than real. Although the armies of Chang Hsueh-liang fought heroically in many instances, neither they nor Chiang's Nationalist armies were in any way equipped to oppose the well-armed, ruthless,

Chinese Boy Scouts protest U. S. appeasement of Japan.

and ably led Japanese mechanized forces. The only possibility of successfully fighting Japan lay in a vast mass uprising of the Chinese people in their hundreds of millions—and such an uprising could only have revolutionary implications. But Chiang Kai-shek had resolutely set his face against any such revolutionary outburst. Instead he concentrated on "uniting" China by continuing his Final Extermination Campaigns against the Chinese Communist forces. All during the years from 1931 to 1937, while Japan continued to encroach upon Chinese sovereignty, Chiang met their expansionism with a policy of appeasement. He had no other apparent choice. Historically, Japan's overt invasion of China is supposed to have started in 1937. But the Chinese-Japanese war commenced in 1931, although only one side (Japan) was fighting it.

In 1932, the Japanese Imperial Navy, perhaps jealous of Japanese success in Manchuria, attacked Shanghai—carefully avoiding the International Settlement, but savagely shelling the Chinese quarters. The Chinese 19th Route Army (a force only nominally under Chiang Kai-shek's control) put up so brave a resistance that the Imperial Fleet had to call upon the Japanese Army to save them from disaster. Even so, the fight went on for more than two months before the outgunned and outnumbered 19th Route Army retreated. Their defiance of the invader aroused students in all the Chinese universities to demand that Chiang declare war on Japan. But the Generalissimo clung to his policy of exterminating Communists while appeasing Japan. The Nationalist government signed a truce with the Japanese commanders at Shanghai whereby Chinese forces were withdrawn from the city while the Japanese garrison remained.

In 1933, Japan invaded the Chinese province of Jehol in the north. They conquered an area of 100,000 square miles in a campaign that lasted ten days—through the use of motorized forces and swift-moving armor. The military lessons of this campaign were not lost upon the German observers present, who were thereby encouraged in the development of their own *Blitzkrieg* tactics. Japan, clinging to her policy of slicing up China piecemeal and under various disguises, did not attempt to annex Jehol for herself. Instead the province was annexed by the Japanese puppet state of Manchukuo. Nationwide indignation swept China, and Chiang was again urged to declare war on the national enemy. But once again he capitulated, signing an agreement with Japan which recognized the conquest of Jehol.

"The Chinese 19th Route Army (a force only nominally under Chiang Kai-shek's control) put up so brave a resistance that the Imperial Fleet had to call upon the Japanese Army to save them from disaster." Chinese machine gunners await the Japanese in the streets of Shanghai.

From Jehol the Japanese were now well placed to infiltrate into the Yellow River region of north China. This they proceeded to do —but not in a directly military way. Instead they undermined Nationalist control of the area. First a campaign of large-scale smuggling was introduced—with the smugglers under the protection of the Japanese Army. Thousands of tons of cheap Japanese goods flooded the north China market where they undersold Chinese products. In addition, this flood monopolized foreign trade in the area and replaced it by imports (illegal of course) on which no import duty was paid to the Nationalist government—thereby further weakening Chiang Kai-shek's regime. Once economic chaos had been established, the Japanese insisted that order in the area could be maintained only by "councils" of Chinese who were "acceptable" to the Japanese High Command. Kuomintang offices and government agencies, as well as personnel, were to be withdrawn from Peking, Tientsin, and the other large cities of north China. A semiautonomous buffer region was to be created—first step toward Japan's outright annexation of the whole area. Chiang Kai-shek's government swallowed even this bitter pill. Through a series of agreements signed with Japanese officials in 1934 and 1935, Japanese domination of north China was accepted.

But Chiang Kai-shek and his government were not the Chinese people—in fact, as we have seen, they were in some respects very far removed from the vast masses of their countrymen. The popular indignation against Japan, usually led by China's politically astute students, gathered increasing momentum. And now it was fed by the continuing hatred of the people of Manchuria and north China for their cruel conquerors. Demonstrations multiplied in major Chinese cities such as Shanghai, Canton, and Nanking itself. Tens of thousands of Chinese workers went out on strike against Japanese-owned mills, mines, and businesses throughout China. Acts of sabotage occurred daily in the north and in Manchuria.

The Chinese Communist reaction against Japanese aggression had been clear-cut. The Soviet Republic of China (while it was still based in Kiangsi Province, before the Long March) had simply declared war against Japan. One of the stated objectives of the Long March had been to bring Communist armies to a point from which they could fight the Japanese, and the Long March was made under the slogans: "Chinese must not fight Chinese!" and "Resist Japan!" In this policy they were faced by a strangely "split" outlook on the part of the Soviet Union. Ever since Chiang Kai-shek's suppression of the Communist Party and subsequent break in relations with Russia in 1928, Stalin had followed a policy of supporting the Chinese Red armies (though this support was entirely platonic, since no Russian supplies of any kind could possibly reach Mao Tse-tung and his followers), and denouncing Chiang Kai-shek as a "fascist beast." But by 1934 the Russian leadership was becoming increasingly concerned that Germany and Italy might one day attack the Soviet Union. Furthermore, the European dictators were busily sounding out military leaders in Japan with the longe-range objective of enlisting her aid against Russia. Resistance to the Japanese therefore seemed more desirable to Stalin's government. But in China only Chiang Kai-shek could possibly organize meaningful resistance —if he could be persuaded to do so. So the Soviet Union found itself in the anomalous position of trying to establish new relations with Chiang Kai-shek with the object of supporting him in real resistance to Japan, while at the same time Chiang was continuing his endless campaigns against the Chinese Communist Party, also nominally supported by the Soviet Union.

The complications, divided councils, and growing frustration of different factions in China culminated in a bizarre incident which came to be known as the "Sian Kidnapping." It had its roots in the determination of Manchurian troops driven from their homeland by the Japanese to fight their way back. When the Red Army reappeared in Shensi Province after its fabulous Long March, it was in close proximity to the Manchurian forces of Chang Hsueh-liang who had been driven from their homeland in 1931. These troops, and their commander, had never given up the fight against

"Demonstrations multiplied in major Chinese cities. . . ."

Chinese students perform an anti-Japanese street-play in Shanghai.

Japan. But they had been forbidden to take direct action by Chiang Kai-shek. Furthermore, they had been deployed by Chiang Kai-shek to contain the Red Army. But now that they were neighbors of Mao Tse-tung's forces, it was quickly apparent to Chang Hsueh-liang that the Reds were sincere in their determination to fight Japanese aggression—and that with their aid, there was a fighting chance for victory. Chang Hsueh-liang asked for, and received, instructors from the Red Army to train his men in the deadly guerrilla warfare of which the Communists had become masters. More and more the Manchurian troops were not only refusing to heed Nationalist orders to campaign against the Communists, they were actually allying themselves with Mao's Red Army. The problem became one of discipline to the Nationalist government at Nanking. In December, 1936, Chiang Kai-shek flew personally to the town of Sian, Manchurian headquarters, to confront the rebellious troops.

When Chiang arrived at Sian he found open mutiny. Both the Manchurian commander, Chang Hsueh-liang, and his men refused to follow orders to attack the nearby Red armies. Instead they demanded that Chiang lead the entire nation in a war of liberation against Japan. The Manchurians arrested Chiang Kai-shek and it seemed only too likely that they would execute the Generalissimo on the spot. Tension mounted. Chiang refused to make any kind of deal with men he considered "mutineers"—and the Manchurian tempers were growing short. But two factors saved the situation.

First of all, Madame Chiang Kai-shek prevented the all-out Nationalist attack on Sian which was being urged by various Kuomintang generals. Instead she herself flew to Sian to join her husband in captivity. The moral force of this example of courage deeply impressed the Manchurian soldiers. Secondly, and more important, Mao Tse-tung (on the advice of Stalin) hurriedly dispatched Chou En-lai to Sian to talk Chang Hsueh-liang out of executing his prisoner. For Stalin (and Mao too) wanted a united front against Japan—and without Chiang Kai-shek to head it, such a front was inconceivable. The final outcome of the kidnapping was dramatic.

Chiang Kai-shek was unconditionally released. Not only that, but Chang Hsueh-liang accompanied the Generalissimo back to Nanking to voluntarily stand trial for insubordination. He was to remain a prisoner of Chiang Kai-shek for the next thirty years—and was still under "detention" in Formosa in 1967!

The "bizarre incident" at Sian had enormous repercussions. The greatest was the realization that swept through the Chinese people that if the moral prestige of Chiang Kai-shek's position as Chief of State was so great that he was inviolate even among his enemies, then China was truly coming of age politically. It meant the end of the long and bitter civil war between Communists and the Kuomintang. It meant that China could turn to face Japan as a united nation. A great wave of patriotic fervor arose throughout China after Sian. And the implications of all this were not lost upon the Japanese.

Six months after the Sian incident, Japanese troops at the Marco Polo Bridge on the outskirts of Peking opened fire on Chinese guards. The date was July 7, 1937. What followed was, for many years, referred to by Japanese militarists as "the China Incident." But in China it came to be known as the Great Patriotic War. To history it was the opening battle of World War II.

8

The China Incident

THE JAPANESE, of course, had no way of knowing that they were breaking open a hornet's nest. Japanese soldiers had killed many a Chinese customs guard before, had staged many a petty "incident" as an excuse for further encroachment upon China. The Marco Polo Bridge shooting was intended merely as a prelude to the seizure of power in north China by Japanese stooges among the higher Chinese officials in the area. But the Japanese did not reckon with a new factor in the situation—the newly born determination and confidence which had spread among the common Chinese soldiers after Sian. When the Japanese opened fire, Chinese soldiers shot back—in spite of the fact that they were poorly equipped and ineptly led. The result was confusion and, when the Japanese brought heavy artillery and mechanized forces to bear, slaughter. Once started, the Chinese resistance spread rapidly. It could not be wished away, covered up, or quickly destroyed. The Japanese timetable of subversion in north China was delayed until only full-scale war could gain them their objectives. It was a war which was to last for eight years and bring to an end Japanese militarism.

In the summer of 1937, still hoping to localize the fighting, mislead the outside world, and provoke dissension in Chinese ranks, the Japanese insisted that the fighting was only an "incident"—and for the next few years they were to continue to refer to the huge land and sea campaigns they waged against China as the "China Incident."

The nature of the Chinese response to this incident was dramatically demonstrated at Shanghai. This city, it will be remembered, had successfully resisted the Japanese Imperial Navy's assault in 1932 when only Chiang Kai-shek's policy of appeasement caused the withdrawal of local Chinese forces. Perhaps still smarting from that fiasco, the Japanese fleet determined that it would now take Shanghai by frontal assault. Accordingly, in the fall of 1937, the Japanese massed cruisers and destroyers, moored off the city, and opened a tremendous naval bombardment of the Chinese quarters (the International Settlement was, of course, sacrosanct). They were aided by heavy air raids. Then, with the city afire and resistance presumably crushed, naval marines landed to seize control. But they quickly found that every burning building was a small fortress that had to be taken by assault. Chinese troops had withstood the naval gunfire as well as the aerial bombardment and remained to exact a very heavy toll of the overconfident Japanese marines. Vicious street fighting developed. It was soon apparent to the Japanese command that the Imperial Navy was once more about to lose a battle at Shanghai. Finally, in desperation, regular army forces were landed in overwhelming numbers. Even so, it took Japanese forces almost three months to subdue Shanghai and break through the Chinese lines around the city.

The quality of the fighting at Shanghai electrified all China and deeply alarmed the Japanese Imperial Staff. Never had Chinese troops fought so ferociously before. Unfortunately, in Europe and

America the amazing doggedness with which Chiang's troops defended Shanghai was ascribed more to Japanese inefficiency than to Chinese determination. It was only several years later, when British and American forces reeled beneath Japanese blows, that the courage and resourcefulness of Chinese resistance became apparent to the West.

While the Japanese were battering against Chinese resistance during the summer and fall of 1937, the new United Front between the Kuomintang and Communist parties, for which Mao Tse-sung had called and which Chiang Kai-shek promised at Sian, came into being. After several months of Kuomintang-Communist negotiations, Chou En-lai was appointed vice-director of the Political Department of the Chinese Army by Chiang. Yeh Chien-ying, who had been the Red Army chief of staff, became head of the Kuomintang's new school of guerrilla warfare. The Red Army was now incorporated in the Nationalist forces as the Eighth Route Army (though it retained semiautonomous status), and command of the Communist areas was given to Chu Teh, Mao's army commander, within the framework of overall Nationalist control. Kuomintang prisons now released thousands of Communist and Liberal intellectuals to join in the fight against Japan, while the formerly dreaded Nationalist secret police devoted less time to murdering Chinese Liberals and Communists and more time to assassinating Chinese who collaborated with Japan in the conquered areas. The people of China, united at last, gave Chiang Kai-shek more support than any other Chinese ruler had enjoyed for many centuries. Without that unity and that support, it is doubtful if China could have survived the disasters which now crowded upon her.

The Japanese had already seized Peking, Tientsin, and other north China cities during July, 1937. With the collapse at last of Chinese resistance at Shanghai later in the year, Japanese mechanized and armored forces were now able to break out into flat, open country where their mobility and firepower gave them a tremendous advantage over the ill-armed Chinese forces opposing them. Furthermore, the Japanese enjoyed complete air supremacy. Their bombers and fighters were able to range at will over Chinese lines and cities without any opposition. Perhaps of even more decisive importance, the Japanese Imperial Navy was able to navigate the Yangtze River, thereby outflanking successive Chinese defense lines.

After the fall of Shanghai, Japanese forces fought their way up the Yangtze to Nanking, the Nationalist capital. There, at the end of 1937, they surrounded the Chinese garrison and smashed it—Chiang Kai-shek's government had already fled far inland to the city of Chungking, where they were to remain for the duration of the war. When Japanese troops entered Nanking in the winter of 1937, they ran amok. Civilian men, women, and children were massacred in an orgy of rape, killing, and destruction. Perhaps incensed at continuing Chinese resistance, and perhaps because Nanking had been modern China's capital, the Japanese High Command gave the city over to their troops for nearly a month of ferocious plunder. Over thirty thousand Chinese were killed in what soon became known throughout a shocked world as the "Rape of Nanking." But if this bestial behavior was intended to cow the Chinese, it had exactly the opposite effect—all China became inflamed with hatred of the invaders and resistance stiffened even more. Furthermore, public opinion in the Western democracies (so often underestimated as a force in world affairs) universally condemned the Japanese barbarism and began to pressure the British and American governments into extending aid to Chiang Kai-shek.

Nor did the Japanese invaders win all the battles. In the north the Eighth Route Army under Chu Teh began to infiltrate Shansi Province—both to establish a base for guerrilla operations against

NEXT PAGES: *"When Japanese troops entered Nanking in the winter of 1937 they ran amok. Civilian men, women, and children were massacred in an orgy of rape, killing, and destruction."*

the Japanese and to test the nature of the Japanese forces in the area and the people's will to resist. In September, 1937, they came into contact with two Japanese divisions. In the pitched battle which followed, the Japanese divisions were utterly destroyed and the Eighth Route Army helped itself to much needed weapons and ammunition from their fallen foes. And to complement this Communist victory in the north, Nationalist troops at Taierhchwang administered a major defeat to Japanese forces who were attempting to press on from ravaged Nanking. The determination of Chinese resistance could be measured by the scorched-earth policy they now adopted, which included not only the destruction of factories and mines and food supplies before the advancing Japanese, but also the opening of the great Yellow River dikes to flood thousands of acres of crop land.

The problem of conquering China seemed, to the Japanese, to rest upon communications. They needed China's railroads, waterways, and ports to maintain a large mobile army. Therefore, during 1937 and 1938, Japanese forces concentrated upon seizing port cities, inland capitals, and, above all, the railroads. Before overwhelming firepower the great port cities fell, one by one: Canton, Amoy, Tsingtao; the inland capitals, such as Hankow and Soochow; and the areas around the railroads and rivers which linked these cities. By the end of 1938, despite bitter Chinese resistance, most of coastal China, of north China, and of the strategic areas behind the coast were in Japanese hands. And these regions contained practically all of China's industries and communications. It seemed impossible that Chinese resistance could continue. Yet Chiang Kai-shek, in a decision which must be reckoned as one of his greatest contributions to Chinese history, decided to continue the war.

The Nationalist armies on the regular front had fought well against the Japanese. But their tactics, largely learned from German military advisers, were orthodox and rigid. Against a much better equipped enemy they had little chance of success. As time went on, Nationalist armies, although they fought willingly enough,

found themselves more and more on the defensive. They occupied fortified positions, waited for the Japanese to attack—and hoped they would not. But the regular front, as the Japanese were to learn to their sorrow, was not the only front in China.

The second front against Japan in China was a nationwide guerrilla campaign waged by Communists and non-Communists alike. Although guerrilla areas were often under the leadership of members of Mao's Red Army, many were under independent leadership and all fought as United Front units. While regular Nationalist armies fought a traditional "positional" war against Japan, these guerrilla bands, which grew to be sizable armies, fought according to the tactics Mao Tse-tung had developed during the civil war and Long March; they were as successful against the Japanese as they had been against the Kuomintang.

Early in 1938, small units of the Red Army (now the Eighth Route Army) began to infiltrate areas behind the Japanese lines. They marched at night, using evasive tactics learned during the Long March, avoiding enemy strong points. When they reached regions which had good geographical possibilities for guerrilla warfare, such as mountains or heavy forests, or areas where the people had already organized anti-Japanese guerrilla units, they established themselves and began raiding local Japanese garrisons, breaking communication lines, and even fighting battles with small Japanese units. The bases established during this early period of the war became the nuclei of the so-called Liberated Areas. It is worth noting that from 1938 to the end of the war in 1945, the Japanese never succeeded in conquering completely any of the Liberated Areas and in most were reduced to sitting apprehensively in garrison towns and wondering where the guerrilla forces would strike next.

The best known of the Liberated Areas (because it was the one most visited by foreign newsmen) was the Shansi-Chahar-Hopei Base, encompassing a huge part of the hinterlands south of Peking and Tientsin. The emergence of this Liberated Area furnishes a good example of how resistance behind Japanese lines came into being. Anti-Japanese warfare in the Wutai Mountain Range in the northwest of this area was commenced by a handful of men (not more than two thousand) belonging to the Red Army's 115th Division, led by General Nieh Yung-chen, a Communist veteran, in alliance with the former Nationalist magistrate of the village of Wutai, Sung Shao-wan. Meanwhile, in the hills west of Peking itself, bands of patriotic students and intellectuals (very few of them Communists), who had fled Peking when the Japanese captured the city, began to mobilize the peasants of the area. They were helped in this task by small remnants of Chang Hsueh-liang's shattered Manchurian Army. Arms were acquired by attacking and wiping out small Japanese outposts or were gathered from the peasants, many of whom had long kept rifles to protect themselves against bandits. On the broad and fertile central Hopei plain it was a regiment of Manchurians (who, instead of following the retreat of their army, stayed behind to organize guerrilla warfare) around whom the resistance crystallized. They were joined by smaller units organized by students, retired military officers, local Communist agents, and even in some cases by landlords and local police forces. And although the central Hopei plain was admirably suited to motorized and mechanized warfare, during a seven-year struggle the Japanese were never to conquer it.

Gradually the small pockets of resistance in this area established contact with one another as their activities expanded. Gradually, too, the invaluable experience of the Communists during the civil war brought them into positions of leadership. As early as October of 1937, a conference of delegates from all resistance forces in the region was held at the town of Fuping. Here the guerrilla representatives voted to adopt Red Army methods of warfare and of organizing the peasants for the struggle—while at the same time maintaining strict autonomy in the internal administration of their various units. Thus, with the establishment of a central command, the Shansi-Chahar-Hopei Liberated Area came into being as a unified front composed of many different political elements whose principal objective was simply to fight Japan.

In December of 1937, at a meeting in the village of Wutai, political administration of the Liberated Area was organized. Adopting suggestions put forth by Communist representatives, it was decided that *all* anti-Japanese political parties would be allowed to operate freely in the region. All the residents, both men and women, who were not actually helping the Japanese were to be allowed a free and secret vote in elections. Furthermore, rents in the area were to be lowered twenty-five per cent, and the land of traitors was to be divided up among the poorest peasants. A bank and other means of economic control were organized to purchase supplies and to fight against smuggling. Sung Shao-wan, the Kuomintang magistrate from Wutai, was elected chairman of the Liberated Area, presiding over a council on which Communist, Kuomintang, Liberal, and nonparty groups were represented. The new administration of the Shansi-Chahar-Hopei Liberated Area was recognized and approved by Chiang Kai-shek's representative, General Yen Hsishan, commander of the Second War Zone.

The story of this Liberated Area was repeated in region after region behind Japanese lines. In spite of the maps which showed Japanese penetration in solid colors in Western newspapers, the Liberated Areas soon became huge expanses of countryside in which millions of people lived and fought.

One of the last of the Liberated Areas to be established during the first two years of war was in the Yangtze River valley. Here the many small units of the Red Army which had not gone on the Long March but had taken to the mountains of Kiangsi, Fukien, and Hunan provinces gathered together to form the New Fourth Army (named in memory of the Fourth Army in which Kuomintang and Communist troops had fought side by side during the revolutionary campaigns of 1927). The mobilization of these Communist units was, at first, opposed by local Kuomintang leaders—and, when the New Fourth Army was finally established, it found itself operating under far different conditions from those obtaining in Eighth Route Army areas. The Eighth Route Army was based in the Communist provinces into which it had moved at the end of the Long March, and could therefore organize Liberated Areas according to Mao Tse-tung's principles, but the New Fourth Army, under direct Nationalist control, operated in an area in which the hatreds and feuds of the civil war were still raw and under political restrictions imposed by the Kuomintang. They could not, for example, organize and arm the peasants or reduce rents or divide up the land of traitors, but were forced to conduct their activities along more or less strict military lines. The New Fourth Army operated along the Japanese-held railroads between Nanking and Shanghai and around Hankow.

In 1938 Chiang Kai-shek made a number of speeches in which he outlined a new military policy for the regular front armies. Since these forces could not defeat the heavily armed Japanese in pitched battles, they would adopt a new method of fighting known as "magnetic warfare." When Japanese forces advanced, Kuomintang units would retreat slowly, keeping up a constant harassment of the enemy. Thus the Japanese would be lured far from their supply bases while at the same time their main units would be weakened by the necessity of leaving small garrison parties behind to protect their supply lines. When the advancing Japanese were sufficiently extended and sufficiently weakened, Chinese armies would converge to destroy them. This was, basically, a policy of trading space for ultimate victory, but China had plenty of space. Although it was to lead to several notable victories later in the fight, magnetic warfare left the initiative largely to the enemy. If the Japanese refused to advance, it could not be practiced.

By the end of 1938 the Japanese were, in fact, refusing to advance. They had already won control of practically all of China's cities, her railroads, her industry, and her coastline. There was little profit to be had by carrying the war into the vast hinterlands of the country. Besides, Japanese militarists, emboldened by the success of Hitler and Mussolini in winning "bloodless" victories over England

*"This was, basically, a policy of trading space for ulti-
mate victory, but China had plenty of space." Chiang
Kai-shek and military advisers plan their campaigns.*

and France during the era of appeasement, were now thinking in
terms of conquering a huge east Asian empire to extend from
Manchuria to Australia. The "China Incident" was to be terminated
by peace negotiations if possible or carried on as a limited "holding"
war. This basically defensive policy in China, coinciding with
Chiang Kai-shek's inability to wage offensive warfare, led during
1939 and 1940 to a stabilization of the regular front.

If the Japanese could not or would not expend the force necessary to completely conquer China, Chiang Kai-shek by no means had the force to defeat them. If the Japanese were to be driven from China it would have to be with the aid of foreign powers—and Chiang, watching his country bleed under the Japanese occupation, was not very particular about which foreign powers they were to be. Friendly noises were made in Great Britain and America which sent Red Cross and other aid to the embattled Chinese, but Chiang could not help but note that the United States and Britain continued to sell huge quantities of oil, scrap iron, and other raw materials to Japan, without which her war machine would have speedily collapsed. The Soviet Union, in line with Stalin's policy of supporting anyone who would keep Japan occupied in the Far East, sent war materials in small quantities and Russian technicians to advise on their use. They also sent a force of five hundred fighter planes (and pilots) to fight the Japanese in the skies over Hankow and Chungking. For the sake of unity and in an attempt to soothe Kuomintang suspicions, Russia sent no aid at all to Mao's Red Army forces.

By 1939 it was becoming apparent that the Western democracies were neither able nor willing to stand up to Hitler's Germany. The Munich Pact, by which Britain and France abandoned the republic of Czechoslovakia to the Nazi dictator, served notice on Chiang Kai-shek that he could expect no help from the West in his fight against Japan. Furthermore, the sudden announcement of the Nazi-Soviet Non-Aggression Pact in August of 1939 meant that Russia also would abandon China to her fate, since Japan was an ally of Germany. Soviet advisers and the fighter planes were, in fact, withdrawn late in 1939, though Soviet supplies continued surreptitiously to enter China. It was obvious that the united front against fascism in Europe had crumbled; what hope therefore could there be for a united front against Japanese imperialism in Asia? Then, with the Allied defeats during the first year of the European war, it seemed clear that Germany would emerge as the most powerful nation in the world—and probably the only one able to effectively extend help to Chiang Kai-shek in his struggle to free China.

German advisers had helped build Chiang's Kuomintang armies. They had developed Nationalist strategy against the Communists during the civil war years. And in spite of the fact that Japan was nominally Germany's ally, Nazi agents in Nationalist-held territories and in the capital at Chungking whispered to Kuomintang leaders that Germany was invincible and would, as soon as the European war ended, settle Japan's hash in Asia speedily. It seemed plausible to the embattled Nationalists that an alliance with Hitler's Germany was their only hope of driving out the Japanese. The price of that alliance would have to be the destruction of Communist influence in China—in other words a renewal of the civil war between Kuomintang and Red armies. That such an inter-Chinese bloodletting could only help the Japanese seemed less important to some Kuomintang officials than their fear of the social revolution both implicit and overt which was going on in the Red-dominated guerrilla areas.

For by 1939 the alliance between Kuomintang and Communists which had been so joyously proclaimed two years earlier was showing signs of strain—and its progressive decay was not due to German influence or considerations of "Grand Strategy" alone. Many other factors, some inevitable, some not, were leading to a new break between Chiang's government and Mao's forces.

First of all, by their retreat to the hinterlands, the Nationalists were removed from the progressive forces centered in China's cities. Their retreat was one which took place in time as well as space. The economic base of the Nationalist struggle was now almost entirely founded on the backward villages of western China which were themselves still immersed in semifeudal conditions. To mobilize peasant strength, the conservative and landlord-dominated Nationalist government could only operate on traditional and, basically, exploitive lines in the villages. Thus, instead of turning land over to peasants and organizing them into their own armies, Kuomintang officials could only increase taxes and conscript men in the age-old way. To do anything else would be to duplicate the Communist guerrilla methods which were revolutionizing the areas in which they operated. But such a policy was entirely against Kuomintang philosophy.

Secondly, when the Japanese adopted a passive attitude in their war in China, immediate pressure against Nationalist armies was relieved. The new Japanese policy seemed to be to alternate savage air attacks against Chungking with peace proposals to the Kuomintang. And in their occupied areas, the Japanese found the inevitable percentage of traitors to help them set up puppet regimes—traitors who often had strong ties to members of Chiang's government. The terrible pressures of the early days of the war which had forged the Kuomintang-Communist collaboration were now greatly lessened. Nationalist leaders began to think once more of how they could establish their authority over Red Army-dominated areas.

Finally, amid the maze of conflicting advice, hopes, fears, and intrigues generated by the European war, Chiang Kai-shek concluded that it was safer to wait and see which side won. While he would accept help from any source, he would not commit himself either diplomatically or militarily until the international situation clarified.

In early 1939, the Kuomintang had purged the political department of the National Military Council which had been formed to give direction to Nationalist-Communist cooperation. Chou En-lai, the Communist vice-chairman of this council, was stripped of all but decorative functions. Meanwhile, student and intellectual-led army propaganda teams were either dismissed or reorganized under tight Kuomintang control. The Kuomintang secret police turned once again to raiding book stores, arresting students, assassinating intellectuals, and terrorizing "leftists." Travel and communication between Nationalist areas and the Red armies in the north as well as the New Fourth Army region were gradually cut off. The supply of Nationalist arms to the Eighth Route Army and other Communist forces was abruptly halted. Police cordons were thrown around Red Army areas—and these cordons were gradually built up into a total military blockade in which hundreds of thousands of Chiang

Kai-shek's best troops were employed—at the expense of the front against Japan.

The collision course between Kuomintang and Communists finally exploded in the "New Fourth Army Incident" of January, 1941. The claims and counterclaims of both sides in this affair have yet to be fully clarified. Basically the importance of the New Fourth Army to both Chiang Kai-shek and Mao Tse-tung was the fact that it operated in and controlled large parts of the countryside around Shanghai and Nanking—China's most modern and highly developed region. Both Mao and Chiang could foresee that in the event of eventual Chinese victory over Japan, control of this area might be decisive in any struggle for power between them. In any case, in late 1940, the Nationalist high command ordered the New Fourth Army to leave its Liberated Area and concentrate north of the Yangtze River in Eighth Route Army territory. New Fourth Army commanders protested the move. The Eighth Route Army had requested no reinforcements and their departure would mean the return of a large and vital region to Japanese occupation. Furthermore, they were unprepared for a long march to the north through enemy-held territory. The Kuomintang's will prevailed, however, and in January, 1941, the New Fourth Army marched north, leaving behind only its base establishments, such as corps headquarters, military schools, hospitals, etc., with about eight thousand combat troops to protect them. When these units started north in the footsteps of the main forces, they were suddenly attacked by Nationalist troops. The noncombat personnel suffered heavily. Doctors, nurses, political agitators, headquarters staffs, and cadets were killed or captured. But New Fourth Army combat forces, which had mostly crossed to the north bank of the Yangtze, escaped relatively unscathed. The New Fourth Army lost about three thousand in killed or captured personnel, while inflicting (according to Communist sources) nearly twenty thousand casualties on the Nationalists.

But the losses suffered by either side in this brief encounter were of much less importance than the effect of it on Nationalist and Communist strategy. The Communists recognized the New Fourth Army Incident as the opening gun in a new civil war—a civil war which could only bring disaster to the war against Japan. In a reappraisal of policy, Communist leaders decided that they would withdraw entirely from the Kuomintang government at Chungking—but would not wage war against it. On the other hand they would prepare for further Nationalist attacks on their forces while continuing the guerrilla war against Japan. The New Fourth Army was taken over by Communist staffs and assigned a new area of the anti-Japanese front. The Nationalists, who might now have moved in force against the Red armies, were restrained—partly because even the most reactionary Kuomintang officials recognized the suicidal nature of such an effort in the face of Japanese hopes, and partly because news of the New Fourth Army Incident had reached the outside world. Britain and the United States, anxious to keep China effectively fighting Japan, expressed their concern to Chiang Kai-shek and brought to bear what pressure they could in the cause of Chinese unity.

On the surface, therefore, China remained united, at least against Japan. But both Nationalists and Communists were now determined to place their own interests first, so that if open civil war did break out, they would be well prepared for it. Communist troops continued their aggressive harassment of the Japanese in the Liberated Areas, Kuomintang troops continued their defensive holding operations on the regular front, both sides kept a wary eye on each other, and both sides jockeyed for political advantage. But these uneasy maneuverings, schemes, and intrigues were suddenly and dramatically complicated on December 8, 1941—the day (east of the international date line) on which Japan commenced her suicidal war against the West, the day on which China, after four years of heroic resistance, found herself no longer standing alone.

9

The Dragon's Teeth Are Sown: 1942-1945

IN CHINA the first result of the Japanese attack on Pearl Harbor was that the government of Chiang Kai-shek declared war against Japan! Until December, 1941, after many years of bitter fighting, there had been no state of war declared between the two combatants —and this paradox was only the first in a war which was to be full of paradoxes, a war which developed in totally unexpected ways. One of the greatest paradoxes of the Pacific war was that China, where more than a million Japanese troops were supposedly locked in mortal combat with almost five times their number of Nationalist soldiers, was to become known as the "Inactive Theater of Operations." Aside from the ever-expanding guerrilla war against Japan in the Liberated Areas, and a few large battles fought almost in desperation on the regular front, the beginning of the Anglo-Amer-

177

ican war against Japan signaled the end of meaningful hostilities in China.

To the Chinese—both Nationalist and Communist—the beginning of Japan's war against Britain and America came as a deliverance. The entry of the Western democracies as China's allies was greeted with unalloyed joy in Chungking. Now Japan would speedily be brought to ruin, vast quantities of supplies would flow to China's armies, and, in spite of the fact that Britain and America were allied in Europe with the Soviet Union, the Communist influence in China would somehow be reduced. None of these expectations was to prove realistic—and the first of them to go was the hope of a quick Japanese defeat.

To Chungking's horror and amazement, the Japanese swept all before them in the first months of the Pacific war. Hong Kong, Singapore, Manila, the Dutch East Indies, Malaya, Burma, Borneo, and the seas between were conquered by Japan with remarkable ease. Chinese troops had held out against overwhelmingly superior Japanese firepower at Shanghai for three months: British troops surrendered the mighty fortress of Singapore in a matter of days. The high and mighty imperialist nations were being chased from their bastions by mere Asiatics in a most humiliating way. No matter what the eventual outcome of the war, it was certain that the Western powers would never again enjoy their former prestige in Asia. The fate of Hong Kong, the great port city which the British had wrested from China early in the nineteenth century, is illustrative.

Late in 1941, when the threat of war had become obvious, Chungking (in the person of Madame Chiang Kai-shek) had offered to send as many as a full division of soldiers into Hong Kong disguised as students, policemen, etc., to help the British defend their colony in case Japan attacked. This was not entirely altruistic. Hong Kong, although blockaded from Nationalist China, remained an important port and manufacturing center from which some supplies were still being smuggled to Nationalist forces. More than that, Nationalist leaders, including Chiang Kai-shek's family, had large deposits in

Hong Kong banks and investments in certain of the city's industries. Chinese elements of the population of Hong Kong also volunteered to form defense detachments. Communist agents in Hong Kong offered plans to cooperate with British troops from the nearby East River Guerrilla Base—one of their Liberated Areas where they had been powerful for the past three years.

The British reaction to all these proposals was an excellent example of the hangover of outmoded ways of thinking about Asia which, to a certain extent, still afflicts some Western nations. Basically, it was rooted in a grand contempt for the military abilities of both Japanese and Chinese. No yellow men had ever yet defeated white troops (somehow or other the Japanese victory over Russia in 1905 didn't count) and none ever would. Besides, mobilizing the strength of Hong Kong's two million Chinese (there were only sixteen thousand non-Chinese in the colony, including all British troops) meant getting involved in politics—and any kind of political movement among colonial people would have revolutionary overtones. As a gesture toward British-Chinese unity in the coming struggle, fifty Chinese were allowed to join a special Chinese regiment where they received much less pay than British soldiers and were not allowed to rise above the rank of sergeant.

Hong Kong would, no doubt, have fallen to Japan in any event —it was much too small an area and too weakly held to hold out for long against the preponderant Japanese power which could be brought to bear. But the manner and duration of its fight might well have taken a decidedly different turn. As it was, British troops, fighting with stubborn bravery, were completely helpless in the face of modern Japanese infiltration tactics. The thousands of Chinese who might have fought at their side were not invited to the battle —and it was all over in a few days. British soldiers who escaped capture made their way in small groups to the East River Liberated Area only a few miles from Hong Kong, where they were taken under the protection of the battle-hardened guerrilla troops. These same guerrillas penetrated the Japanese lines around Hong Kong after the city's fall and without much difficulty gathered up many of the thousands of weapons abandoned by the defeated British.

The story at Singapore and in Burma was much the same. Only at Bataan and Corregidor was a protracted defense made—largely because the Filipino people were allowed to fight for their own country.

The inability of many British and American military commanders and diplomats either to understand or accept the changes wrought by war and revolution among the people of Asia was to plague the Allied war effort in continental Asia. It finally led to a series of disasters and crises which continues to threaten world peace to the present day. The dragon's harvest of war and hatred which the West is still reaping in Asia was sown during the Second World War.

Anglo-American defeats in the early months of the Pacific war only intensified the Kuomintang's determination to avoid battle against Japanese forces and hoard men and supplies against the time when, if Japan won, they could be used as bargaining counters in peace negotiations, or if the Western powers won, they could be used in renewed civil war against the Chinese Communists. Besides these calculations there was the hard fact that American aid, which had begun to trickle into China over the famous Burma Road, was now abruptly cut off.

The Burma Road, a miracle of engineering, had been constructed during 1937-1938 under American supervision by thousands of Chinese laborers whose primary tools were their hands. It snaked seven hundred miles through jungles and over precipitous mountains from Rangoon in Burma to Kunming in southern China. With the Japanese in control of China's coastline, it was almost the only way American supplies could reach Chiang Kai-shek. To defend this vital route, several American-trained Chinese regiments were rushed into northern Burma in 1942 to join British and local forces in opposing a massive Japanese invasion of that country. They were under the command of the man who had trained them, Gen-

General Joseph Stilwell

eral Joseph Warren Stilwell, an American military adviser who spoke Chinese, understood Chinese history, and sympathized with the aspirations of the Chinese people. The title "Vinegar Joe" was affectionately bestowed on him by his men for his habit of speaking his mind both forthrightly and bitingly. Unfortunately, Vinegar Joe and his troops only arrived in time to share in the general debacle in Burma. But the determined general led his forces on foot in a grueling march out of the Burmese jungles which won the attention and admiration of the world. After the fall of Burma, American supplies had to be flown in from airfields in northern

India over the "hump"—the Himalayan Mountain Range, accurately described as the Roof of the World. General Stilwell himself, appointed chief of staff to Chiang Kai-shek, was supposed to train the Chinese Army, build up American forces and supplies so that American bombers could one day attack Japan from Chinese bases, and reopen the Burma Road or build a new one. That these tasks were clearly beyond the capacity of the Nationalist armies, no matter who commanded them, did not deter Vinegar Joe from doing his best.

Another American commander on the spot was Colonel (later General) Claire Lee Chennault, who in early 1941 had formed the American Volunteer Group of fighter pilots to fight for Chiang Kai-shek. This band of experienced fliers, surreptitiously supported by the United States government in the months before Pearl Harbor, was ostensibly a group of mercenaries, fighting in Nationalist China's employ. Taking the name "Flying Tigers" from the tiger's teeth painted on the fuselages of their planes, these men built up a tremendous record of Japanese planes shot down over Burma and southern China. With American entry into the war they were transformed into the nucleus of the 14th United States Air Force, still under General Chennault's command.

The discrepancy between American plans for Chinese participation in the Pacific war and Chiang Kai-shek's views on the subject became more and more pronounced as time went by. It was reflected in the deteriorating relationships between Chiang and Generals Stilwell and Chennault. Basically, the United States hoped to achieve three things in China: to keep up Chinese active resistance so that large numbers of Japanese troops would continue to be pinned down; to open and operate airfields capable of handling not only fighters, but also the huge B-29 long-range bombers which were expected to pulverize Japanese cities; and, when conditions warranted, to transform the Chinese theater of war into a great base for the assault on the Japanese home islands. An integral part of this last plan was, of course, the massive destruction of both the huge

Japanese land forces in China and their crack armies in Manchuria. For the most part these hopes and plans were to remain completely unfulfilled—and a mighty factor in their disruption was the decay and demoralization of the Nationalist government in China during the war years.

With the American victories at Midway and the Coral Sea, the Russian victory at Stalingrad, and the British victory at El Alamein, it soon became clear to the Kuomintang government that Japan would be defeated in any case. Why, therefore, should China expend any more lives and strength than the minimum necessary in the struggle? As ultimate victory was assured, it appeared of growing importance to Chiang Kai-shek (who had, on American insistence, been named Supreme Commander in the China Theater of Operations) to conserve his best (American) trained troops for the coming civil war against the Communists rather than "waste" them fighting the Japanese. American military observers estimated that between 200,000 and 400,000 of the best trained, best (American) equipped Nationalist troops were employed in manning the cordon which Chiang had thrown around the Communist-dominated areas in which the Eighth Route Army and other forces continued their guerrilla campaign against the common enemy. With the relaxation of Nationalist war efforts came demoralization which infected the Kuomintang government from top to bottom and quickly spread among troops and officers in the field.

In early 1942, the United States announced that it would lend $500,000,000 to Nationalist China to support her war effort. But no controls could be exercised over how this money was to be spent. A tremendously high proportion of it found its way into the pockets of government officials in the form of bribes and graft. Nor did

NEXT PAGES: *"For the most part these hopes and plans were to remain completely unfulfilled. . . ." A train carries refugees from the Japanese offensive of 1944.*

this financial injection do anything to alleviate the plight of the Chinese peasant, who was still heavily taxed by the Chungking government to support the war. Rich Chinese, who were usually also government officials, exported their money for safekeeping to American and Swiss banks. Kuomintang fiscal policy, which was both confiscatory and corrupt, soon led to widespread inflation, which bore most heavily on the poor while it further enriched the wealthy. Trading with the enemy and smuggling became common phenomena among higher Kuomintang government and army officials as the value of goods increased. In the meantime, the heavy Kuomintang land taxes, combined with increasing rents due to inflation, were quickly and effectively wiping out the middle class of Chinese peasants—those who owned their own land more or less free from debt. Investigators reported that the number of "middle peasants" had been reduced in many provinces from forty per cent to twenty per cent between 1939 and 1942—and thereafter the rate skyrocketed. While a small handful of these landowning peasants found their way into the wealthier classes (usually by black marketeering), the overwhelming majority of them were reduced to landless beggary and joined the swelling ranks of the poorest classes.

An excellent example of the progressive decline of Kuomintang honesty, efficiency, and wartime morale was dramatically provided by the great famine of Honan Province in 1942 and 1943.

The fertile and populous Honan plain is the center and, in many ways, the strategic heartland of China. Its people are hardy and have farmed the area through successive dynasties, Mongol and Tartar invasions, and civil upheavals for more than three thousand years. When the Kuomintang forces conquered the province in 1927, their nationwide victory over warlordism was all but assured.

From 1938 to 1940 the Japanese had been penetrating the province, their troops occupying strategic cities and towns but leaving the countryside very much alone. Chiang Kai-shek had sent strong government forces under General Tang En-po to garrison those sections of Honan into which the enemy had not yet driven. These

Kuomintang armies were welcomed by the peasants, and although they fought few battles against the Japanese, it was felt that their presence kept Japan from conquering the entire province. It soon developed, however, that the army of Tang En-po had no intention of ever offering battle. Instead they developed a flourishing trade with enemy forces—especially through the unoccupied "no man's land" town of Chieh-shou. War was forgotten while profiteering and black marketeering became a way of life for officers and land-lords who had sufficient capital to engage in it.

To accumulate such capital, Tang En-po's officers and the local landlords respectively kept raising taxes and rents. New taxes were invented so that every time the peasants slaughtered a pig, gathered grain, or even dried fruit on their farmhouse roofs, they had to pay something to Tang En-po.

Then, in 1942, the crops failed. Floods, drought, and early frost ruined the harvest. In many places only twenty per cent of what had been sown could be reaped. But the tough peasants of Honan pulled in their belts and figured that if they ate just enough to keep alive they could last through the year until the next harvest. Then the tax collectors came, as usual. They had been instructed to collect taxes at an even higher rate than in the past, and no nonsense about it. If the peasants were unable to pay in grain, then they would have to sell their farm animals or implements or, more probably, the farm itself, to local moneylenders and landlords. Of course these worthies were now offering less per acre of land than what that acre would produce in a single year. But the peasants had no choice. They sold their land for a pittance.

The people of Honan began to starve. They ate grain husks, grass, and leaves. Sometimes they ate "mercy earth," a kind of dirt which, while it has no nutritional value, at least gives a feeling of being full. In some villages leaves were being sold at five dollars a pound. Finally, those who were more fortunate were forced to eat their farm animals. Soon the sight of thousands of peasants trudg-ing the roads in search of food became commonplace. When they

tried to drag themselves into neighboring provinces in which food supplies were normal, they were turned back by cordons of Kuomintang troops and police.

Then, in the spring of 1943, the new crop appeared in the fields. However, as soon as it was ready for harvest a great plague of locusts descended upon it and destroyed it completely. The roads of Honan became littered with the skeletal corpses of the dead. Trees throughout the province were stripped of their bark to just the height a man might reach. American newsmen who visited the area calculated that more than three million people had died of starvation between the spring of 1942 and the summer of 1943—and the great dying was not yet over.

Chiang Kai-shek himself and Kuomintang officials in prosperous Chungking at first tried to deny that any famine was taking place. But news of the true state of affairs could not be suppressed. Relief funds from the United States which now began to pour into China were diverted to the pockets of Kuomintang officers of the central government—only a small fraction of American aid ever reached the starving peasants of Honan. When the Communist-dominated Liberated Areas of Shensi and Yenan announced that they would take in refugees from Honan, supply them with seed, and set them to farming wastelands, Kuomintang forces on the Honan border machine-gunned crowds of starving peasants trying to break through. Nevertheless, under international pressure, Chiang Kai-shek announced that the central government would remit taxes in Honan for the following year—when, presumably, most of the taxable peasants would be dead in any case. Later on Chiang also passed a law which permitted any peasant of the area who had been forced to sell his land at a low price to buy it back at that same price. Unfortunately, the overwhelming majority of peasants who survived were illiterate and could never hope to advance any claims against the powerful landlords and moneylenders.

The ultimate result of the Honan famine became apparent in 1944. In that year Japanese forces resumed their offensive in the province. Tang En-po's demoralized and corrupted army made not the slightest effort to stop them. And, as small units of his army dispersed into the hills, they were set upon by the vengeful peasants, who beat them to death and took their weapons.

The progressive decline of Kuomintang prestige during the war years (remarkably similar to the ancient "loss of heaven's mandate" of the older dynasties) and the increasing certainty that Japan would be defeated by American forces in any event, led Mao Tse-tung and his followers to reach certain conclusions. Their continuing guerrilla warfare against Japan in the Liberated Areas was diminishing as Japanese forces showed less and less inclination even to attempt to conquer Red Army-dominated regions. On the other hand, the Kuomintang's policies throughout the territories under its control were steadily building up revolutionary pressures among the peasants. Sporadic revolts had already erupted behind Kuomintang lines. Mao's problem, as he saw it, was to win over the sympathies of these desperate peasants and, at the same time, prepare for the inevitable day when civil war would again break out between his own and Chiang Kai-shek's forces—after Japan's defeat. To meet these problems it was necessary to develop a self-sufficient "rear area" which could support itself despite the Kuomintang blockade and from which Red armies could draw strength; to prepare to win control of those areas from which Japanese troops would one day withdraw (especially the coastal cities and the industrial northeast, Manchuria); and to tighten Communist Party discipline as a necessary step toward ultimate victory.

Party discipline was enforced through a series of lectures, meetings, and decrees in which a program of "thought reform" called *Cheng-feng* was initiated early in 1942. It was aimed at convincing Mao's non-Communist liberal allies among China's intellectual and student classes that they must associate themselves more intimately with the toiling peasants—get their hands dirty—with the ultimate aim of converting them to Communist doctrines. Furthermore, those who would not submit to a tighter party discipline were to be expelled. Greater care was also to be exercised in recruiting new party members to make certain that no "defeatist" elements entered. Direct and hostile propaganda against the Kuomintang was to be undertaken throughout China and, where possible, foreign nations. This last part of the program commenced early in 1943 when Russian news agencies began printing denunciations of the "defeatist" and "corrupt" policies of the Kuomintang regime and its leader, Chiang Kai-shek. Although such attacks were designed to serve Communist ends, they were difficult to deny for the simple reason that they were often largely true.

Of greater importance to Mao's program, however, was the transformation of the Liberated Areas into self-supporting and loyal bases for the Red Army. It was not Mao's aim to "communize" these regions—his party needed the support of middle-class intellectuals, landlords, and students for the time being, and the United Front among all classes was still in effect. But the worst aspects of peasant life were to be abolished or ameliorated. Rents were reduced to a tolerable level and rent control was rigidly enforced—but landlords' estates were not seized or turned over to the tenant peasants. And while the landlord was forbidden to raise rents or evict peasants, the peasants were obliged to pay their reduced rents, and if they did not, landlords could call on Mao's government for help in collecting. Control of the villages was taken out of the hands of the richest inhabitants and given over to councils. Delegates to these councils were elected by all villagers, to whom a vote was now guaranteed. Taxes were reduced and placed on a progressive scale—the poorest peasants paying little or nothing, while the richest landlords paid as much as thirty per cent. But there were no "special taxes" or arbitrary impositions inflicted on the rich, who paid less under Communist domination than they had lost to the corrupt and haphazard Kuomintang warlords and officials in the past. Of course, in the long run, Communist policy would be to eliminate the landlord class entirely. But for the present they were content simply to regulate land and village affairs with a view to making life livable for the poor as well as the rich.

In order to win peasant loyalty to the Red Army (and incidentally to increase production of food), Mao had long since inaugurated the policy of having those regiments which were not engaged in fighting plant their own food on wastelands and help the peasants to gather harvests. Red Army horses were turned over to local villagers for plowing between battles, and Red Army soldiers toiled side by side with the peasants in the fields. So strict was Mao's rule about not imposing more of a burden on the peasants than was absolutely necessary that even the top Communist leaders had to plant gardens of their own. Chu Teh, Red Army commander-in-chief, planted lettuce, which he tried (with mixed success) to introduce as a staple crop in Yenan, while Mao himself (a chain smoker) planted tobacco. There could be no question that Mao's "get your hands dirty" policy did more than any amount of Communist propaganda to win peasant support. The idea that an army did not necessarily have to bring disaster to their lives but might even help them raise their standard of living was a revolutionary thought to China's peasants. The fact that Red Army units in their village would give them tools, horses, and willing hands to help did more than anything else to weld peasants and army together in support of Mao's programs.

Visits to Red Army Liberated Areas by American newsmen and military intelligence officers (visits which Chiang Kai-shek could not fully prevent) led to a growing conviction among the visitors (and through them to the outside world) that China's true resistance to Japan was centered there. And, furthermore, that if the Kuomintang government did not change its policies quickly and decisively, it would lose any subsequent civil war with the Communists. Observing life among the peasants in these regions at a time when Mao's policy was that of enlisting the cooperation of all the people, including landlords and gentry, many foreign observers assumed that Mao Tse-tung and his followers were no more than "agrarian reformers." This was by no means true. They were dedicated Communists as fully committed to an eventual Socialist revolution as any Communist Party anywhere. The confusion arising from the lack of information and contact between Mao's party and the outside world was to have disastrous repercussions in the postwar world.

There was still another interested party in China at that time—Japan. For if an uneasy truce had prevailed for years along the regular front between Kuomintang and Japanese forces, events of the Pacific war now determined the Japanese high command to break it. American forces were slowly but surely forcing the Japanese back throughout 1942 and 1943. By 1944 it was clear that the final battles would be fought on Japanese soil and that ultimate defeat for Hirohito's armies could not be avoided. There was, according to Japan's military counsels, only one hope of averting final disaster. That was to make the price of conquering Japan so high in terms of potential casualties that American leaders would prefer to end the war by negotiation. To accomplish this end it would be necessary to convert China into a huge bastion of Japanese power, manned by millions of dedicated soldiers who could engage large American forces in an endless land war. In order to accomplish this it was now necessary both to defeat the Kuomintang armies on the regular front and to crush out resistance in the Liberated Areas. As a bonus of this campaign, the American airfields from which the 14th United States Air Force operated in China would fall into Japanese hands.

The new Japanese offensive in China was launched early in 1944. Within a few months it had succeeded in conquering practically all of south China, smashing Kuomintang armies with unexpected ease and driving United States air power from its bases into the remote hinterland. Chiang Kai-shek's entire military effort seemed likely to fall to pieces and there were many who expected China to drop out of the war altogether. Only in the Liberated Areas did Japan meet such determined resistance that her campaign not only failed, but Red Army units advanced to seize coastal areas from

NEXT PAGES: *"Chiang Kai-shek's entire military effort seemed likely to fall to pieces. . . ."*

which Chinese forces had been excluded for years. By the end of 1944, according to the Japanese themselves, seventy per cent of their military effort in China was directed in a losing battle with Mao's semiguerrilla forces, while only thirty per cent was expended against Chiang's regular troops.

The Japanese offensive in China brought American-Chinese relations to the point of crisis. General Stilwell, it will be remembered, had been directed to prepare China as a great staging area for the Allied assault on the Japanese home islands. Much money, effort, and blood had been spent in that attempt. Now, when five years of stalemate and corruption on the part of Chiang's government, combined with the Japanese offensive, brought all Vinegar Joe's hopes to nothing, his cup of bitterness spilled over. For years he had tried vainly to introduce some sort of order, some spirit of resistance, into Chiang's armies. He had seen his best troops marched off to contain Communist forces in the Liberated Areas rather than to fight the Japanese. He had seen American supplies, flown in at such great cost in men and planes over the Himalayan Mountains, wasted and openly sold by profiteers. He had seen the airfields built by thousands of Chinese coolies with their bare hands given up without a fight by demoralized Kuomintang forces. The hatred he had grown to feel for Chiang Kai-shek was demonstrated by the fact that in his diaries Stilwell never failed to refer to the Generalissimo as "peanut." To Stilwell it was clear that if Chinese resistance was to survive the Japanese offensive, Kuomintang forces would have to cooperate with Communist troops. American supplies would have to be sent into Red Army Liberated Areas. More than that, control of China's war effort would have to be wrested from corrupt Kuomintang officials and generals. General Stilwell, having for years reported conditions in China as he found them, now requested that the American government bring pressure to have him appointed Supreme Allied Commander in China.

The negotiations which followed, the investigations undertaken by several American "missions" to Chungking and into the Liberated Areas, the conflicting advice received by Washington from its representatives, the pressures brought to bear by Chiang Kai-shek's government in Chungking and Washington, the resultant rifts and discords of American policy in China, culminated during the war years with the dismissal of General Stilwell as Chiang Kai-shek's chief of staff and his replacement by General Albert C. Wedemeyer. All this belongs to the story of China's postwar years and will be dealt with in the next chapter. Here it is sufficient to point out that, although an American observer group was sent to Yenan to cooperate with Mao's Red Army, American policy remained concentrated in the effort to win a victory through and with the Kuomintang forces of Chiang Kai-shek and to support him against all domestic opposition whether Communist or not.

The Japanese offensive, which was renewed in 1945, continued to make progress almost at will against Kuomintang troops, and continued to fail against the Liberated Areas. But the fate of Japan in China was to be decided by events elsewhere. At the Yalta Conference in February, 1945, the American government, at the continued urging of the American chiefs of staff who were, quite properly, worried about the expenditure of American manpower that a long campaign against Japanese forces in China might entail, secured the Soviet Union's agreement to enter the Pacific war three months after the war in Europe should end. The price of Russian help in the Pacific was to be the return to Russia of those Far Eastern possessions wrested from her by Japan in 1905. Obviously the Russian target would for geographic reasons have to be Japanese forces in Manchuria and north China—a fact which would bring her armies into close contact with Mao Tse-tung's Red Army. On the other hand, American pressure at Yalta induced the Soviet Union to recognize Chiang Kai-shek's government as the only legal government in China, an agreement which was formalized by the Chinese-Soviet Treaty, signed on August 14, 1945, just as the Pacific war came to its end. But by that time, the Soviet Far Eastern Army, which had easily crushed all Japanese resistance in its path, was already in possession of Manchuria.

In the end it was American sea power and air power which brought Japan to defeat. But the terrible explosions over Hiroshima and Nagasaki which brought the Second World War to a close and opened even more frightening prospects for the future sounded in China more like the starting gun for a new civil war.

10

Red Star Ascendant

FROM 1946 until late in 1949 one of the largest wars of modern times was fought in China. Although the superficial currents of the struggle viewed in terms of political maneuvering, diplomatic angling, propagandistic charges and countercharges seemed hopelessly tangled to Americans, the deeper tide of China's renewed civil war ran in the same plain channel it had followed since 1928. A corrupt, inefficient, and exploitive government—the Kuomintang regime of Chiang Kai-shek—had lost the confidence of the overwhelming majority of the Chinese people—and nothing on earth could prevent them from trying to overthrow it. China was going to move out of its semifeudal past with or without outside aid. The fact that this movement was controlled and directed by the Chinese Communist Party may have been painful to Americans. But the question might have been put: what alternative did America now offer to promote the emergence of the Chinese people from thousands of years of misery along democratic, non-Communist lines? Unfortunately, the only answer that could be made to this question was that we continued to support Chiang Kai-shek's government—a government which even the most conservative of American observers condemned as dictatorial and backward. Nevertheless, American support for Chiang Kai-shek was an important theme of the civil war which was now to be fought between Kuomintang and Communist forces across the face of China.

Jockeying for strategic and tactical advantage in the renewed civil war began as soon as the Pacific war against Japan ended. Japanese commanders in China's cities and provinces received orders from the Kuomintang government to surrender only to Nationalist representatives and troops. Under no circumstances were they to surrender to the forces of the Liberated Areas. To disarm the former enemy, and occupy the great cities of Shanghai, Canton, Peking, Tientsin, and Mukden, Chiang Kai-shek's forces were rushed there in American planes and ships. It was estimated that the American air-sea lift transported more than 500,000 Nationalist troops during the last part of 1945—to places from which they could recommence Chiang Kai-shek's endless Final Extermination Campaigns against Mao Tse-tung's Red Army and the Liberated Areas.

Part of the forces moved by American planes and ships was Chiang's famous New Army. This force, composed of more than thirty divisions (of which twelve were United States trained and equipped) had been carefully hoarded by Chiang during the last stages of the Japanese war. Now they were to be deployed against the Chinese Red Army. Nor with the end of the Pacific war did American aid to Chiang cease. Planes, tanks, guns, and munitions

"Japanese commanders in China's cities and provinces received orders from the Kuomintang government to surrender only to Nationalist representatives and troops." Chiang Kai-shek re-enters liberated Nanking.

flowed at an ever-increasing rate into Kuomintang ports. The number of American military advisers attached to the Nationalist forces did not diminish but rather increased to the number of one thousand. It was estimated that aid to Chiang Kai-shek during the year 1946 alone amounted to more than a billion dollars. In addition, American forces were stationed at Shanghai, Tsingtao, and other port cities where the United States Navy had anchorages and where Chinese technicians were trained at United States army and naval schools. Before seeing what Chiang Kai-shek accomplished with this aid, it would be well to find out why he received it.

General Stilwell's concern over the lack of unity during China's war against Japan had found echoes in the United States government. Accordingly, in June of 1944, Vice-President Henry Wallace, accompanied by a large staff of technical experts, arrived in Chungking to urge cooperation between Nationalist and Communist forces against the common enemy. At his insistence Chiang Kai-shek allowed an American military observer mission to proceed to Mao Tse-tung's base in Yenan and remain there for the duration of the war. Aside from the enthusiastic reports this mission forwarded to Chungking and Washington regarding the Red Army's military efforts in the Liberated Areas, it was apparent that despite American promptings, both Nationalists and Communists would continue to expend much of their energy watching each other rather than fighting Japan.

On a more direct level, the United States Ambassador to China, Patrick J. Hurley, continued to urge Chiang Kai-shek to reform his government. It was in return for Chiang's promise to undertake widespread democratization of his regime that General Stilwell was recalled (his acid tongue and frankly expressed contempt of the Kuomintang regime had earned him the reciprocal hatred of Chiang Kai-shek) in 1944 and replaced by General Albert C. Wedemeyer, an officer whose views Chiang found much more acceptable. The fact that Chiang Kai-shek did not keep his promise to liberalize and rationalize the Kuomintang government (which, considering its

Chiang Kai-shek

composition and basis of power, might well have been beyond his abilities in any event) did not affect continued American support.

The truth of the matter behind the complexities of opinion seems basically to have been that by late 1944, many Americans, including Ambassador Hurley and General Wedemeyer, had become concerned with the potential danger of conflict between Soviet Russia and the United States in the post-World War II era. An increasing amount of evidence was accumulating that Stalin and his government intended to wage a cold war of fraud and force against American interests throughout the world as soon as "peace" was re-established. And in such a struggle the position of China would be vital. There was a strong current of opinion among United States representatives in China that Chiang Kai-shek had to be supported no matter how disgraceful his regime, simply to keep China from falling into the Russian sphere of influence. That such support, short of a full-scale war fought by American troops, was bound to fail was not always apparent to American representatives, who were too often abysmally ignorant of recent Chinese history. Nor were matters helped by American war weariness in 1945. Having fought a global war for four years, the American people wanted only to demobilize and dismantle their tremendous war machine as quickly as possible. They were not interested in the complexities of rights and wrongs behind a new civil war in faraway China. During the war years Chiang Kai-shek had been built up as a great hero of the anti-Japanese struggle by Allied propagandists—continued support of his government seemed only reasonable to a basically disinterested public in the United States. Also, it must be said that certain American business and manufacturing interests whose investments in China depended on the continuance of Chiang Kai-shek's regime had for some years maintained a political "lobby" in Washington which attempted to influence American policy. The so-called "China Lobby" was notably well financed and from 1945 to 1949 remarkably successful in urging ultimately disastrous policies on the United States government. But of course the primary mistake of American views on China after World War II was the idea that *any* American policy could basically influence the future history of a subcontinent of 450,000,000 people, whose ancient culture was utterly remote from the American experience.

While the United States supported Chiang Kai-shek, it became Russian policy to support Mao Tse-tung. This represented a sharp departure from Stalin's prewar decision that the Chinese Communist Party had small prospects of success against the Kuomintang and

Mao Tse-tung

his wartime support of Chiang's government. It was basically dictated by many of the same considerations which moved American leaders but in reverse or mirror-image of United States policies. Thus while United States ships and planes rushed Chiang's armies back to the coastal cities, Russian forces in Manchuria facilitated the entry of Chinese Communist troops into the areas under their control. Although Mukden, Manchuria's largest industrial city, was occupied by Chiang's forces, much of the Manchurian and north China countryside came under the domination of Mao's Red Army.

Although Russia supplied no weapons to Mao's troops, Soviet commanders made sure that captured Japanese materiel was turned over to Chinese Communist forces. In return, Mao Tse-tung made no protest against the Russian seizure of factories and industrial establishments in Manchuria. It has been estimated that from twenty to thirty-five per cent of Manchurian industrial resources were dismantled and shipped to Russia as "reparations" during 1945 and 1946. The fact that these establishments were Japanese-owned did little to obscure the fact that this Russian action (against which the United States protested fruitlessly) delivered a crippling blow to China's postwar economy.

A final American effort to bring peace and order to China was made by General George Catlett Marshall, former United States chief of staff, in December of 1945. Against a background of increasing skirmishes between Nationalist and Communist troops throughout China, especially in the north, General Marshall sought to find a political settlement which would prevent an all-out civil war. Since the only possible road to peace was to introduce Communist representatives into the Chiang Kai-shek government (representatives, it will be recalled, who would be speaking for more than 100,000,000 Chinese), General Marshall proposed that a constitutional coalition government be formed. Chiang Kai-shek would remain as President of the Chinese Republic, both the Koumintang and Red armies would be drastically reduced—and the entire pill would be coated with heavy American economic and financial aid. In January, 1946, a combined Political Consultative Conference held at Chungking reached a political agreement between Kuomintang and Communist deputies. A cease-fire order was issued to both armies. In February a merger of the two forces was agreed upon. Under the supervision of truce teams made up of American, Kuomintang and Communist representatives, the fighting stopped. This

"A final American effort to bring peace and order to China was made. . . ." General Marshall meets with Chiang Kai-shek and Madame Chiang.

accomplishment was in itself a tremendous tribute to the personal integrity and capability of General Marshall—but it lasted only a few weeks. When, in January, 1947, General Marshall left Chungking, his mission a failure, he issued a report in which he stated:

> The greatest obstacle to peace in China has been the complete, almost overwhelming suspicion with which the Chinese Communist Party and the Kuomintang itself regard each other. . . . On the side of the National Government, which is, in effect, the Kuomintang Party, there is a dominant group of reactionaries who have been opposed, in my opinion, to almost every effort I have made to influence the formation of a genuine coalition government. . . . This group includes military as well as political leaders. . . . Though I speak as a soldier, I must also deplore the dominating influence of the military. . . . The dyed-in-the-wool Communists do not hesitate at the most drastic measures to gain their ends. . . . Now the Communists have broken off negotiations. . . .

In the battles which now spread and multiplied between Chiang's troops and Mao's Red Army, the inevitability of Chiang's downfall was soon apparent. Kuomintang military policy, despite the presence of American advisers, had not changed from the days of the unwritten truce between Nationalists and Japanese. Lacking any broad popular support, Chiang's armies tended to huddle in the large cities and await attack behind fixed defenses. Kuomintang generals, often beyond the control of the central government, tended to hoard their supplies and avoid battle until they could see which way the tide of victory would go. In cases where these generals submitted to Kuomintang direction, they often found that the smallest details of battalion deployment were being dictated to them by Chiang Kai-shek himself, although the Generalissimo was hundreds of miles from the scene of action.

The Communists on the other hand showed that they could adapt their strategy to new situations. At first, while Kuomintang troops with their heavy American armaments held the predominant force, the Red Army followed its traditional modes of guerrilla warfare, maneuvering speedily over open country, recruiting peasants in its path, and avoiding pitched battles. But as Communist forces came into possession of more and more American arms, which they captured from Nationalist troops or which were turned over to them by deserting Nationalist divisions, they showed increasing willingness to fight large-scale battles on traditional lines—and great skill in doing so. Concentrating their strength initially in Manchuria and the north, Communist forces cut off Nationalist troops occupying the smaller cities and forced their surrender, one by one.

American military observers were continually dismayed by the lack of fighting spirit among Chiang Kai-shek's well-equipped troops and by the fact that entire Nationalist divisions often deserted *en masse* to the Red Army or surrendered after only token resistance. But they should not have been so surprised. Chiang's forces were composed overwhelmingly of peasants—the same kind of peasants who formed the backbone of Mao's Communist armies, and the same kind of peasants who had for so long suffered beneath Kuomintang exploitation. The appeal of Communist policies which had successfully attracted support from the peasants in the Liberated Areas was no less to the peasants of Chiang Kai-shek's army. Nationalist soldiers could see no benefit in fighting for a government which oppressed them, and, when given the opportunity, they deserted by the tens of thousands to the Communist side, taking their weapons with them. By June of 1948, Communist forces finally equalled Nationalist forces in numbers of men, rifles, and heavy artillery. In October they were able to force the surrender of the cut-off Manchurian garrisons; on November 1, 1948, Mukden, industrial capital of Manchuria, fell into their hands. From this point on, Mao Tse-tung's armies went over to a national offensive against which Chiang's forces were unable to stand.

Nor was the Nationalist collapse merely military. Behind Kuomintang lines, in the large cities and throughout the countryside, economic chaos mounted. Between 1946 and 1948 prices doubled sixty-seven times. In an attempt to control this galloping inflation, the Nationalist government commenced a currency reform in August, 1948, introducing price controls and seizing private hoards of gold and foreign currency—thereby turning even the rich city speculators against the Kuomintang government. But these reforms were too little and too late. By the end of 1948 Nationalist credit on the stock exchanges of the world was nil, the Nationalist currency practically worthless. Prices in Shanghai had doubled 85,000 times in six months. Even the prosperous city merchants had been brought to ruin and Chiang Kai-shek's government lost what last shreds of support it had enjoyed. Indeed, as the Kuomintang regime tottered, it seemed that its only allies were to be found in certain American military and commercial circles, not in China.

The United States supported Chiang Kai-shek to the very end— and beyond the end. It was not surprising then that the Chinese people came to associate America with the hated Kuomintang regime. In addition, there had been direct "incidents" between Chinese civilians and United States Marines and other personnel stationed in China. While these incidents were no more than typical of the frictions inevitably generated between troops and civilians in foreign lands, the size and hysteria of the anti-American outbursts they caused were a good measure of how far the United States had sunk in the estimation of the Chinese. Madame Sun Yat-sen, who had long since seen more promise in achieving her husband's goals under Mao Tse-tung than Chiang Kai-shek, but who nevertheless remained a friend of the United States, said in a message to the American people in 1947:

> The present crisis is not a question of who wins, the Koumintang or the Communists. It is a question of the Chinese people, their unity and livelihood. . . . Not party rights, but human rights hang in the balance. The American people, who are our allies and have long been our friends, must be told that the presence of United States armed forces on Chinese soil is not strengthening peace and order among the Chinese people. They must be warned that loans should be given only to a reorganized and truly repre-

sentative government . . . that if America makes it plain that she will not supply munitions or military equipment, there will be no spreading Chinese civil war.

Madame Sun's words went largely unheeded.

Mao Tse-tung's land policy during the war with Japan, as expressed in the laws of the Liberated Areas, had been to allow the landlords to retain ownership of their land, but to control the level of rents they could exact from their peasant tenants. Now, however, as the renewed civil war entered a decisive phase, Mao changed this policy. On October 10, 1948, a new Liberated Areas Land Law was promulgated—a law clearly designed to destroy semifeudal land conditions and to appeal mightily to the peasants in the rear of Chiang Kai-shek's armies. Some of its provisions were:

ARTICLE 1. The agrarian system of feudal and semifeudal exploitation is abolished; the agrarian system of "land to the tillers" is to be realized.

ARTICLE 2. Land ownership rights of all landlords are abolished.

ARTICLE 4. All rural debt incurred before this reform . . is cancelled.

ARTICLE 11. The government shall issue deeds to the ownership of land given to the people and recognize their rights of free management.

As a weapon against the Kuomintang, this new land law was the equivalent of many armies. Peasant uprisings began to occur throughout Kuomintang-held territory in which the rebellious peasants were often joined by Chiang's peasant soldiers and formed small but well-trained and fiercely independent Liberated Areas of

NEXT PAGES: *"Chiang Kai-shek's government lost what last shreds of support it had enjoyed." Nanking's Chinese students demand peace with the Communists.*

their own. The dispatching of Nationalist divisions to "contain" these new pockets of revolution seriously weakened Chiang's main armies.

In November, 1948, one of the greatest battles of modern times opened with the roar of massed artillery (artillery which was American-made on both sides). Chiang Kai-shek, against the advice of his staff and of American advisers, had massed more than fifty Nationalist divisions on the plains around the city of Hsuchang. Since the area was in the basin between the Huai River and the sea (Hai) it was later called the Battle of Huai-Hai. It represented a Nationalist attempt to prevent the eruption of Red Army forces into central China. Although Chiang Kai-shek remained in the city of Nanking, far from the scene of fighting, he insisted on controlling the course of the battle down to divisional level. Communist forces, who controlled the railroads leading north, were able quickly to deploy and surround the Nationalist troops on Hsuchang plain. Four Nationalist armies, about 340,000 men, were thus encircled. Seeking to relieve them, Chiang dispatched 120,000 more troops—including his best American-trained divisions. But this force was also surrounded and trapped some miles south of the main Nationalist armies. After bitter fighting the two Nationalist forces were able to join together to form what Chiang termed a "mobile fortress." But the fortress was anything except mobile; it was trapped behind deep entrenchments and enclosed within a ring of 300,000 Communist troops who battered away at it ceaselessly with heavy artillery. Slowly the Red Army drew its net tighter, until finally the entire Nationalist force was trapped within a six-square-mile area. In late December the Nationalist officers and men still fighting were informed that Chiang Kai-shek now proposed to bomb them himself—to keep their heavy weapons out of Communist hands. This was the last straw. On January 10, 1949, the Nationalists at Huai-Hai surrendered. Of the 550,000 Nationalist troops lost in this battle, the Communists claimed to have captured more than 325,000. The way into central and southern China was open to Mao Tse-tung's armies.

While the Nationalists were meeting disaster at Huai-Hai, Communist forces were besieging Peking and Tientsin. Early in January the Red Army under Chu Teh staged a furious and massive twenty-nine-hour attack on Tientsin, breaking Nationalist resistance, inflicting tremendous casualties, and capturing the city overnight. Shortly thereafter a note was sent to the Nationalist commander of besieged Peking, offering him the opportunity of surrendering and threatening a Tientsin-type attack if he did not. The Nationalists quickly surrendered without fighting. On the twenty-third of January, 1949, Communist troops marched into the ancient capital of China.

In April, 1949, after these notable victories had been won in the north, Communist troops fresh from their victory at Huai-Hai approached the great river barrier of the Yangtze. Foreign observers scoffed at the possibility of a quick Communist crossing of this wide, fast-flowing river. The river ferries had been withdrawn, there were no bridges, and the Red Army lacked the means of throwing pontoon bridges across. Furthermore, any attempt to cross in boats would be blasted by the tremendous artillery barrage of waiting Nationalist divisions on the south bank. Besides—where were the boats to come from? But the Yangtze hardly impeded the onward rush of Mao's troops. As his army paused along its banks, peasants volunteered their sampans by the thousands and Red Army forces crossed over *en masse* against light opposition from the surprised and demoralized Nationalists on the other shore. The Yangtze was the last natural barrier to Communist penetration of south China. Clearly the game was up for the Kuomintang armies. Nanking, the Nationalist capital, was captured in May, then Shanghai, then Canton—to which the Nationalist government had fled—until finally, by midsummer 1949, Chiang Kai-shek's government had been forced to flee to the island of Formosa, under the protecting guns of United States fleet units. Although Nationalist pockets of resistance were to continue in existence until the spring of 1950 (Chungking fell to Red Forces in May, 1950), the Nationalist government of Chiang Kai-shek had

"In the name of the Consultative Political Committee and of the Chinese people, I proclaim the People's Republic of China."

been wiped out on the Chinese mainland—and their prospects on Formosa were, at best, indifferent.

On October 1, 1949, Mao Tse-tung mounted to the balcony of the ancient Imperial Palace in Peking. Crowds estimated at 500,000 people cheered wildly and then waited in hushed silence for his words. His voice trembling slightly, he began to read from a prepared speech: "In the name of the Consultative Political Committee and of the Chinese people, I proclaim the People's Republic of China." To many in the crowd those words were freighted with their life history; from the fight against the warlords in 1927, through the bitter defeats they had suffered at Nationalist hands in the early thirties, the incredible heroism of the Long March, the decade-long war against Japan, and the bloodshed and turmoil of the recent past, victory had been wrung. It was a moment of triumph against all but insuperable odds. The Nationalists had been against them, the Japanese had fought them, the United States had supported their enemies heavily, Soviet Russia had given over the years almost no help—the only resource with which Mao Tse-tung's Communist Party had won its struggle was the increasing support of the Chinese people. That, however, proved sufficient. While many observers both in Peking and around the world wondered what trials might lie ahead for China's suffering millions, what hard paths the revolution might now take, no one could doubt that a long era in Chinese history had come to an end and a totally new China was in the making.

Epilogue:

Dragon Harvest

IN A very real sense the triumph of Chinese Communism was the beginning rather than the end of China's attempt to lift herself into the twentieth century by her boot straps. The announcement of the creation of the People's Republic of China did not magically solve China's pressing problems. The questions of land reform, industrialization, flood and drought control, education—and many others —remained to be answered. How Mao Tse-tung's new regime attacked these problems would determine how long the new government would retain "heaven's mandate." Better than anyone else, Mao Tse-tung knew that his People's Republic could survive only with the widespread support of China's peasants and workers. He was determined to win that support, or, if necessary, to enforce it.

218

This was reflected in the establishment of what the Communists termed the "New Democracy" in China during late 1949 and 1950. Government was carried on by a coalition of parties (twenty-three to be exact)—with the Communists predominating. And Mao's Liberated Area policy of not immediately wiping out the commercial classes was continued. While many of the largest industrialists and bankers had to flee for their lives, smaller capitalists were not molested. Although the government had a controlling hand in all activities from farming to heavy industry, China's economy was allowed to remain partially capitalist. This was necessary, according to Mao, in order to get the country back on its feet after a quarter century of war. But Mao and his followers were in a hurry.

Under the Agrarian Reform Law, adopted in 1950, village landlords became the first of the old controlling classes to be wiped out. Throughout China, landlords' property was confiscated and turned over to local village cooperative societies. These cooperative societies —dominated by the poorer peasants and directed by Communist leaders—distributed seized lands among the landless peasants. On the other hand, dispossessed landlords were also to receive a share of their former property so that they could "reform themselves by hard work." To enforce this policy, tribunals were established in villages throughout China. These "People's Courts" had full jurisdiction. They could impose penalties including the death sentence upon recalcitrant landlords. In practice it was generally those landlords whose past crimes (especially collaboration with the Japanese) had earned the abiding hatred of the villagers who suffered the direst penalties. Free at last to avenge thousands of years of repression and exploitation, villagers often resorted to lynch law against the landlords. But according to some Western journalists, there was evidence to show that the "People's Courts," by ritualizing and channeling the peasants' hatred, saved many landlords' lives.

NEXT PAGES: *"These 'People's Courts' had full jurisdiction. They could impose penalties including the death sentence upon recalcitrant landlords."*

As part of its program to win nationwide support (and maintain that support at fever heat during the trials ahead), Mao Tse-tung's government continued to exploit the theme which had been central to Chinese history for more than a century—nationalism. The government-controlled press and radio and the thousands of Communist Party agitators who flooded the countryside continued to whip up enthusiasm under vividly nationalistic slogans. The European Tai-Pan had long since vanished, his "settlements" and "concessions" and "compounds" only a bitter memory, his imperial pretensions a thing of the past. Thus it was the United States which became the central target for Chinese Communist propaganda: for having allied itself with Chiang Kai-shek's Nationalist regime, for being the world's most powerful capitalist society, for having inherited the mantle (and the problems) of leadership among those Western nations whose imperialistic exploitation of China had been the worst in the past, and, perhaps, simply for being the most convenient hate-symbol against which Mao's government could hope to unite China's masses. The United States was continually pictured as the archenemy not only of China's government but also of her every aspiration, of her very life. How much of this abuse was really believed by China's masses or by Mao's government was difficult to determine. Early in 1950, events dramatically illustrated the growing estrangement of the two nations.

On June 25, 1950, North Korean forces, Russian-trained and Russian-equipped, erupted over the South Korean border and within three days had captured South Korea's capital city, Seoul. The United States, legally and morally bound to support the South Korean government (which unfortunately appeared to be almost as corrupt and undemocratic as China's old Nationalist government had been), decided to actively fight the North Korean aggression. In hopes of preventing the spread of war in Asia and confining the struggle to the Korean peninsula, on June 27, 1950, the United States government informed Chiang Kai-shek's Nationalist regime, now holed up on the island of Formosa, that Nationalist air, sea, or "commando" attacks against the Communist Chinese mainland would not be countenanced. At the same time the United States Seventh Fleet, operating in the south China Sea, would secure Formosa against any Chinese Communist attack. Mao's government immediately seized upon this action as further evidence of intolerable American intervention in Chinese domestic affairs. When, during the summer of 1950, United Nations forces in Korea under the command of General Douglas MacArthur completely routed the North Korean Army, Mao's government issued several warnings that any close approach to the Chinese-Korean border by UN troops might lead to Chinese intervention. The Chinese warnings went unheeded, and just before Christmas, 1950, as MacArthur's forces approached the Yalu River, Korea's boundary with Chinese Manchuria, huge Chinese "People's Volunteer" armies poured across the Yalu to inflict a disastrous defeat upon American and United Nations troops.

Although Mao's government (like the American) did not declare war, and although Chinese forces were styled "People's Volunteers," the Chinese war effort in Korea was carried on by regular divisions of the Red Chinese Army, maintained and supplied by both the Chinese and the Russian governments. Chinese soldiers fought with great skill and tenacity and under able leadership—thereby finally exploding the myth of Chinese military inefficiency. But although Mao's government, perhaps on the basis of its early successes, continually announced that American forces and their "United Nations lackeys" would be pushed into the sea, this feat was beyond their power. Now under command of General Matthew Ridgway, United Nations troops soon regained the initiative, and by June, 1951, with "People's Volunteers" surrendering at the rate of sixteen thousand per month, and the front stabilized around the former North-South Korean border. Russia's representative at the United Nations asked for an armistice on behalf of the North Koreans and their allies. Sporadic fighting was to continue throughout protracted and agonizing negotiations until a cease fire was finally established in October, 1953. While neither the United States nor Red China had been willing to expend the force necessary to win a complete victory in Korea, relations between the two countries seemed to have frozen on a level of mistrust and hate.

While his armies struggled in Korea, Mao Tse-tung proceeded with an ambitious program of industrialization at home. This program would demand a heavy investment of capital (either in money or goods) for the establishment of basic heavy industries such as steel mills, mines, transportation, and power. In spite of heavy aid from Soviet Russia (Russian technicians began pouring into China in 1949), this investment, on the colossal scale required, could come only from China's prime resource—agriculture. But to feed China's millions and still have enough surplus to make a meaningful investment in industry meant rationalizing Chinese agricultural methods. It meant that the tiny plots of individually owned peasant land would have to be combined so that they could be farmed with machines. So the land which had been given to the peasants through the Agrarian Reform Law of 1950 was soon to be taken away by the state. However, unlike Stalin's ruthless collectivization program in Russia during the thirties, the Chinese Communist program was intended to proceed carefully and by stages, only advancing to the next stage when it was clear that a majority of China's peasants were willing to accept it.

Thus, in 1953, the Chinese government inaugurated a drive to establish agricultural producers' cooperatives throughout the country. The land would still belong to the individual peasant, in title, but it would now be "pooled" with other individual holdings into a large-scale cooperative farm on which all the peasants would work and from which each might retain his share of the profits, minus government taxes. By 1956 it was reported that ninety per cent of China's peasant households (110,000,000 households) were members of farming cooperatives. Mao's government admitted that only full-scale collectivization (which meant government ownership of all the land) would eventually enable China to modernize her agri-

culture sufficiently to bring production levels up to Western standards. But it was hoped that several years' experience working in cooperatives would prepare peasants for the eventual loss of their title
to the land. Outright collectivization of the land began in 1957,
with, it was claimed, peasant acquiescence. But whether this step
would ensure that increase in farming efficiency demanded by
China's exploding population level, only time would tell.

China's industrialization, which, unlike agriculture, was to fall
under rigid government ownership and control from the very beginning, commenced as soon as Mao Tse-tung's government was
established in Peking in 1949. But it was only with the announcement of a Five Year Plan in 1953 that progress could be measured
and assessed. According to this ambitious plan, more than fifteen
hundred new factories were to be built. And this plan was itself to
be succeeded by Five, Seven, and even Twelve Year Plans—all
aimed at raising the level of Chinese industry to that of the super-
powers, Russia and the United States, within a foreseeable future.
As the years passed it was difficult for outside observers to gauge
Chinese progress. There were to be much-publicized "Great Leaps
Forward" and "Twenty Years Progress in a Single Day"—and rue-
ful admissions that plans did not always translate themselves easily
into accomplishments. Reports on the progress of Chinese industrialization have been conflicting—but that tremendous progress has
been made was clearly proved by the detonation, in October, 1964,
of the first Chinese nuclear device. Observers have generally agreed
that China's industrial growth rate is rapid, impressive, and formidable—the fastest of any underdeveloped country in Asia.

The natural disasters to which China has been prey for so many
centuries—floods, droughts, and their resulting famines and pestilence—could not be legislated out of existence. But the new gov-

NEXT PAGES: *"So the land which had been given
to the peasants through the Agrarian Reform Law
of 1950 was soon to be taken away by the state."*

ernment showed itself determined to overcome them. An example was the Yellow River Project—a plan for the construction of forty-six "staircase" dams along the course of that mighty river, which would provide flood control, irrigation, reservoirs, and electric energy. Since such construction projects as dams were susceptible to the use of China's greatest asset—the physical labor of millions of peasants—rapid progress was made on their construction—not only on the Yellow but also on the Yangtze and other rivers. The days of recurring flood and drought were within sight of being ended. River developments combined with scientific methods of farming were expected to end famines. But China's huge population (600,000,-000 in 1958) kept far enough ahead of the food supply so that food rationing became a staple feature of Chinese life. Nevertheless, with rationing, the burden was at least fairly shared among all classes of the people. Mass starvation such as the terrible Honan famine of 1943 is probably a thing of the past.

On September 20, 1954, the First People's Congress of the People's Republic of China adopted a constitution. Under Article 2 of this document, all power in China now belonged to the "people." But the people were divided into four classes, according to Maoist theory. There were the working class, the peasant class, the middle class, and the upper middle class. If and when any of these classes was arbitrarily removed from its category of being part of the people, it could become the people's enemy and be wiped out by the "Democratic Dictatorship of the People," as the landlord class had been. Maoist doctrine was to speed the transfer of power as quickly as possible down the scale of classes to the working class and the poorest peasantry. As this transfer went on, other economic groups would slip one by one into the dread category of being "not of the people." Thus, besides being an organic legal code, the new constitution was a means of continuing the revolution. Peking hoped to establish a "model Socialist state" by 1973.

Mao's aim in hurrying the industrialization of his country was not only to provide a decent standard of living for her people—it was also to raise China to the rank of a major power on the international scene. The Communist regime in Peking, with long experience of struggle against the European imperialist powers and Japan, bitter memories of American support for Chiang Kai-shek, even more bitter memories of American successes in the Korean war, was convinced that only the building of a mighty military machine could insure it against foreign attack. In addition, it had inherited Chinese claims and ambitions as old as the Middle Kingdom itself. It was determined to re-establish Chinese authority over those regions, such as Tibet and Inner Mongolia, which had been detached from the old empire during the nineteenth century. Furthermore, China was to be once again supreme in east Asia as she had been in the distant past—east Asia was to be her "sphere of influence." The intrusion of any power—European, American, or even Russian— could only be viewed as a threat to China's vital interests. As early as October, 1950, Communist forces had entered Tibet. In 1958 they put down a revolt in that country and formally reannexed it to China. Peking's determination to reassert its authority throughout the realms of the old Celestial Empire was also expressed by the incursion of its troops into the border regions it shared with India. While Chinese claims to disputed territory were often justified (as even the Indian government admitted), the resort to violence to enforce these claims was an ill omen for the future to China's neighbors.

With the death of the Soviet dictator Joseph Stalin in 1953, relations between China and Russia began a steady decline. During Stalin's lifetime, Chinese Communist policy had generally been to pay lip service to advice from Moscow but to go their own way. If, in fact, Mao Tse-tung had followed Russian advice, he would never have survived the civil war of the early thirties. Nevertheless, a

NEXT PAGES: *Mao's aim in hurrying the industrialization of his country was not only to provide a decent standard of living for her people—it was also to raise China to the rank of a major power....*"

formal recognition of Moscow's world leadership of the Communist movement had always been maintained by Chinese Reds. But the Soviet leaders who succeeded Stalin seemed bent on destroying the myth of Stalin's omniscience and on reaching some sort of accord with the West. Chinese Communists feared a general weakening of the Communist line of world-wide revolution. Like Lenin before him, Mao saw that the fomenting of "people's revolutions" against capitalist-imperialist colonies and regimes was his best defense against renewed foreign attack. The preaching of "peaceful co-existence" in Moscow, the picture of Russian Premier Nikita Khrushchev sitting down to dinner with American millionaires in San Francisco—none of this was calculated to appeal to Peking's revolutionary sensibilities. Furthermore, China did not relinquish her claim against certain Russian territories in central Asia and Siberia. A war of words soon developed between Russia and China which led to the withdrawal of all Soviet technicians from China and the complete stoppage of Soviet aid to Peking. Chinese students were withdrawn from Russia, and the insults and wrangling exchanged between Moscow and Peking became so bitter as to raise the prospect —however remote—of an eventual war between the two nations, an unheard-of nightmare to orthodox Marxists.

But if relations with Russia deteriorated, relations with the United States remained frighteningly close to armed conflict. Central to Chinese hostility against the United States was the continued existence of Chiang Kai-shek's Nationalist government on Formosa, protected against attack by the United States. The island of Formosa, 250 miles long and about 80 wide, ruled by the aging Generalissimo with heavy United States economic and military aid, was the only China recognized by the United States government. Chiang's army on Formosa which was itself slowly succumbing to old age could no longer pose any real threat to the now well-trained, well-equipped, enormous Red Army of Mao Tse-tung. But the continuance of Chiang's regime under American protection was as irritating to Peking as, say, the continuance of Jefferson Davis'

Confederate government on the island of Cuba under English protection might have been to Washington in 1865. Furthermore, with American support and by ever-narrowing votes in the General Assembly, Chiang retained control of China's seat in the United Nations. The possibility of recognizing two legal Chinese governments —one in Peking and one on Formosa—was a suggestion refused as indignantly by Chiang Kai-shek as by Mao Tse-tung.

But international "power politics" continued to be beyond the immediate ken of China's vast peasantry. Old Hundred Names was still there on the land (which was no longer his own), and it was upon his shoulders that the new China would have to rise. How had the Communist victory affected his daily life?

First of all there could be little doubt that Old Hundred Names enjoyed a tremendous material gain over his past. Now there was food; now the landlord was gone; now schools and hospitals proliferated over the countryside (Old Hundred Names's children would be literate); new cultural opportunities in the form of traveling theaters, opera companies, and libraries were becoming available. And as machines, especially agricultural equipment, flowed in growing measure from the new factories, the day's toil became less and less unbearable. Most of the worst abuses of the past had already disappeared. Women were accorded the same rights as men; bigamy, prostitution, child selling, and infanticide had largely vanished. The cities were clean, sanitation was introduced to thousands of country villages, railroads and highway networks were being extended dramatically, and electric power began to appear in the most out-of-the-way rural communities. Bandits, warlords, foreign mercenaries—these were only bitter memories. There could be little doubt that Old Hundred Names enjoyed a security and ma-

NEXT PAGES: *"Its government will apparently continue to enjoy the support of the overwhelming majority of its citizens." Mass meeting to celebrate the government take-over of private industry.*

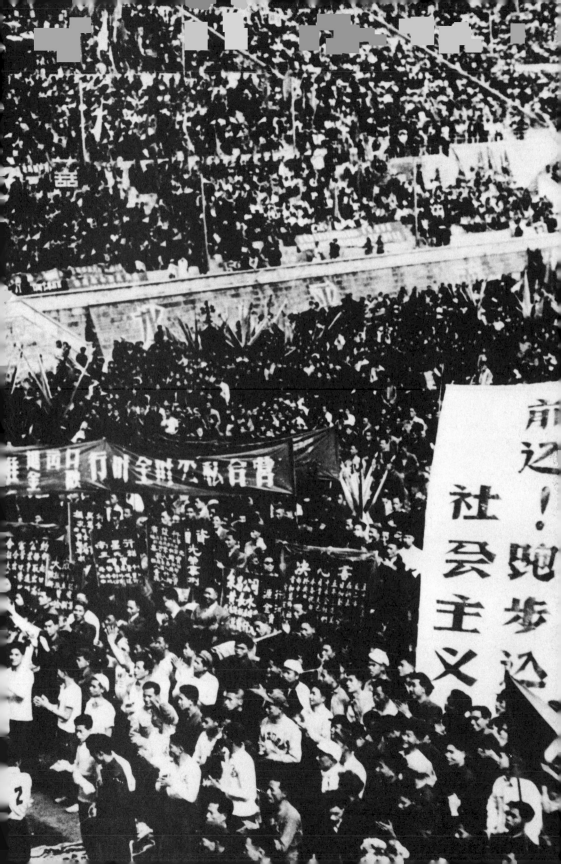

terial well-being such as he had rarely known in all of China's five-thousand-year history.

But what of freedom, of liberty? Old Hundred Names would reply to that question that he now enjoyed freedom from landlords, moneylenders, rapacious armies, and a corrupt government. As for his own participation in politics, he was free to vote yes or no to the approved list of Communist Party candidates to local councils, unions, and associations. If his personal influence at Peking was all but nonexistent, if the Chinese government remained a dictatorship of the Communist Party over the nation, Old Hundred Names had at least become convinced that the party had his best interests at heart.

China's culture had always been authoritarian. The rule of the father, of the landlord, of the government bureaucrat, of the provincial governor or warlord, of the emperor in Peking, had been for centuries the accepted fabric of life. The transfer of authoritarian power to village councils, provincial Soviets, Communist Party bureaucrats, and the party leadership in Peking represented no dramatic change in China's traditions. Political democracy such as is known in Britain or the United States had never existed on Chinese soil (not even under Chiang Kai-shek's regime). Its prospects and possibilities were largely a matter of indifference to Old Hundred Names.

But will it always be so? The Russian Communist experience seems to indicate that as living conditions improve and the strains of forced industrialization are relaxed, people tend to demand greater and greater personal liberties and political freedoms. Only the future can tell if a similar process will gradually ameliorate the Communist Party dictatorship in China as it has in Russia.

In any event, Communist China seems certain to remain a fact of life for the foreseeable future. Its government will apparently continue to enjoy the support of the overwhelming majority of its citizens. And if China, with her huge population, large natural resources, traditional skills, and new sciences ever reached a proportionate standard of industrial power as compared to the United States or Russia, she would be far and away the dominant power on earth.

Whether Americans can accept this approaching fact and live with it is at the root of Chinese-American relations today. In the mid-sixties there were few in the United States who could be found to deny that American policy in Asia had often been mistaken in the past. Americans will have to seek something better than a simple policy of hostility to cope with the new China. At the same time Peking's continued fabrication of hysterical anti-Americanism seems a hopelessly outdated and pointless response to Chinese-American tensions. Whether Chinese and American conduct can now be redirected toward a more realistic and affirmative relationship has become, perhaps, the central problem for the future of both nations. To Old Hundred Names the answer, while of great interest, is not of world-shaking importance. Come what may, he knows he will go on.

Bibliography

A Suggested Reading list will be found
at the end of the Bibliography.

ADLER, SOLOMON, *The Chinese Economy* (New York 1957)
BARNETT, A. DOAK, *Communist China and Asia* (New York 1960)
BELDEN, JACK, *China Shakes the World* (New York 1949)
BELOFF, MAX, *Soviet Policy in the Far East* (London 1953)
BODDE, DERK, *China's Cultural Tradition* (New York 1957)
———, *Peking Diary* (New York 1950)
BOULGER, DEMETRIUS, *China* (London 1904)

BRINE, LINDSAY, *The Taiping Rebellion* (London 1862)

BUCK, PEARL, *The Man Who Changed China* (New York 1953)

———, *All Men Are Brothers* (trans.) (New York 1933)

CALLIS, HELMUT G., *China, Confucian and Communist* (New York 1959)

CHANG, CHI-YUN, *The Essence of Chinese Culture* (Taipei 1957)

CHART, RALPH M., *Chronology of the Chinese Emperors* (New York 1934)

CHIANG KAI-SHEK, *China's Destiny* (New York 1947)

COMPTON, BOYD, *Mao's China: Party Reform Documents, 1942-44* (Seattle 1952)

CREEL, H. G., *Chinese Thought from Confucius to Mao Tse-tung* (Chicago 1953)

CRESSEY, GEORGE B., *China's Geographic Foundations* (New York 1934)

DE BARY, WILLIAM T. (ed.), *Sources of the Chinese Tradition* (New York 1960)

DICKINSON, GOLDWORTH L., *Hands of China (Letters from John Chinaman)* (New York 1932)

DRUMMOND, R., & COBLENZ, G., *Duel at the Brink* (New York 1960)

EBERHARD, WOLFRAM, *A History of China* (London 1950)

ELEGANT, ROBERT, *Dragon Seed* (New York 1960)

EPSTEIN, ISRAEL, *From Opium War to Liberation* (Peking 1956)

———, *The Unfinished Revolution in China* (Boston 1947)

FABER, ERNST, *Chronological Handbook of China* (Shanghai 1902)

FAIRBANK, JOHN KING, *The United States and China* (Cambridge 1958)

FITZGERALD, CHARLES P., *China: A Short Cultural History* (New York 1954)

FORMAN, HARRISON, *Changing China* (New York 1948)

FREMANTLE, ANNE, *Mao Tse-tung: An Anthology of His Writing* (New York 1962)

GALBRAITH, WINIFRED, *The Chinese* (New York 1943)

GELDER, STUART, *The Chinese Communists* (London 1946)

GOODRICH, LUTHER C., *A Short History of the Chinese People* (New York 1951)

GROUSSET, RENE, *The Rise and Splendors of the Chinese Empire* (London 1953)

HAHN, EMILY, *Chiang Kai-shek: an Unauthorized Biography* (New York 1955)

HSU, FRANCIS L. K., *Americans and Chinese* (New York 1953)

HUGHES, ERNST R., *The Invasion of China by the Western World* (New York 1938)

ISAACS, HAROLD R., *No Peace for Asia* (New York 1947)

LANG, OLGA, *The Chinese Family and Society* (New Haven 1946)

LATOURETTE, KENNETH S., *The Chinese: Their History and Culture* (New York 1946)

MAC LANE, CHARLES B., *Soviet Policy and the Chinese Communists* (New York 1959)

MENDE, TIBOR, *China and Her Shadow* (New York 1962)

NEEDHAM, JOSEPH, *Science and Civilization in China* (London 1956)

REMCOURT, A. DE, *The Soul of China* (New York 1958)

ROBERTS, FRANCIS M., *Western Travellers to China* (London 1932)

ROMANUS, C. F., & SUNDERLAND, R., *Stilwell's Mission to China* (Washington 1953 GPO)

SHABAD, THEODORE, *China's Changing Map* (New York 1956)

SMEDLEY, AGNES, *The Great Road* (New York 1956)

SNOW, EDGAR, *Red Star Over China* (New York 1938)

————,*The Other Side of the River* (New York 1961)

TAWNEY, R. H., *Land and Labor in China* (London 1932)

THOMAS, S. B., *Government and Administration in Communist China* (New York 1955)

WALES, NYM, *Inside Red China* (New York 1939)

————, *Red Dust* (Palo Alto 1952)

WALEY, ARTHUR, *The Opium War Through Chinese Eyes* (New York 1958)

WHITE, THEODORE H., & JACOBY, ANNALEE, *Thunder Out of China* (New York 1946)
WILLIAMS, S. WELLS, *The Middle Kingdom* (New York 1904)

Suggested Reading:
General History:

FAIRBANK, JOHN KING, *The United States and China* (Cambridge 1958)

LATOURETTE, KENNETH S., *The Chinese: Their History and Culture* (New York 1946)

Biography:

BUCK, PEARL, *The Man Who Changed China* (Sun Yat-sen) (New York 1953)

HAHN, EMILY, *Chiang Kai-shek: an Unauthorized Biography* (New York 1955)

SNOW, EDGAR, *Red Star Over China* (contains only authorized biography of Mao Tse-tung) (New York 1938)

WALES, NYM, *Red Dust* (contains biographies of Communist leaders such as Chu Teh and Chou En-lai) (Palo Alto 1952)

Fiction:

BUCK, PEARL, *The Good Earth* (New York 1931)
HERSEY, JOHN, *A Single Pebble* (New York 1956)
WHITE, THEODORE H., *The Mountain Road* (New York 1958)

Index

A

Africa, Chinese trading stations in, 19

"Age of Feudalism," in China, 20-21
    See also Chou Dynasty; feudalism

Agrarian Reform Law (1950), 219, 224

agriculture, 24-28; 211

America. *See* United States

Amoy, 42, 72, 136, 164

Analects (Sayings) of Confucious, The, 24

Autumn Harvest Uprising, 118-119

B

Black Dragon Society, 81

Blücher, V. K., 101

Book of Mencius, The, 24

Borodin, Mikhail, 99-101, 109

Boxer Rebellion (1900), 53-56, 73, 82-83

British East India Company, 36, 37, 39

Buddhism, 29, 31

Burma, fall of, 180-182

Burma Road, 180, 182

C

Cambaluc (Peking), 14
    See also Peking; Peiping

"comprador," 70-71

Cantlie, Sir James, 80, 82

Canton, 72, 92, 164
    "Commune," 109-111, 118
    Sun Yat-sen attempts to seize (1900), 82
    Sun Yat-sen regains control of, (1923), 99

245

J

K